PONS

A RECIPE FOR MURDER

Mörderische Kurzkrimis

zum Englischlernen

CONFIDENTIAL

von Dominic Butler

PONS GmbH
Stuttgart

PONS

A RECIPE FOR MURDER

Mörderische Kurzkrimis
zum Englischlernen

von Dominic Butler

Alle in diesem Buch geschilderten Handlungen und Personen sind frei erfunden. Ähnlichkeiten mit lebenden oder verstorbenen Personen wären rein zufällig.

PONS verpflichtet sich, den Zugriff auf die zu diesem Buch gehörige Vokabeltrainer-App mindestens bis Ende 2020 zu gewährleisten. Einen Anspruch der Nutzung darüber hinaus gibt es nicht.

1. Auflage 2018

PONS Online-Wörterbuch: www.pons.eu
E-Mail: info@pons.de

Projektleitung: Majka Dischler
Autor: Dominic Butler
Redaktion: Dorith Herfeld
Einbandgestaltung: Anne Helbich
Logoentwurf: Erwin Poell, Heidelberg
Bildquellen: Umschlag: Edgar and John/Shutterstock; S. 3: (Dominic Butler): Dominic Butler; S. 6-7: (Weltkarte) Tetiana Yurchenko/Shutterstock, (Stecknadel) PONS GmbH; S. 14: Marco Bicci/Shutterstock; S. 21: Guillermo Gallego Lora/Shutterstock; S. 28: Levranii/Shutterstock; S. 37: Stas Moroz/Shutterstock; S. 45: Kent Weakley/Shutterstock; S. 53: ptaxa/iStockphoto; S. 61: bbernard/Shutterstock; S. 70: Carl K/Shutterstock; S. 78: shuter/Shutterstock; S. 88: Airi Pung/Fotolia; S. 99: Taras Vyshnya/Shutterstock; S. 109: Lori Martin/Shutterstock; S. 118: Helen Hotson/Shutterstock
Logoüberarbeitung: Sabine Redlin, Ludwigsburg
Layout: Petra Michel, Gestaltung & Typografie, Essen
Satz: Datagroup Int. SRL, Timisoara

ISBN: 978-3-12-562101-5

AUTORENINFO

Dominic Butler

Dominic Butler stammt aus Nordengland. Er ist Englischlehrer und Schriftsteller. Nach seiner Schulzeit, die er an einer klassischen Grammar School (entspricht dem deutschen Gymnasium) verbrachte, studierte er Film und Literatur an der Sheffield Hallam University. Während seiner Studienzeit arbeitete er in Teilzeit als Gerichtsschreiber am Strafgericht in Sheffield. Dort erwachte sein Interesse für Kriminalfälle, die von nun an Thema vieler seiner Kurzgeschichten wurden. Dominic lebt und arbeitet zurzeit in Ungarn, wo er Englisch unterrichtet und gerade seinen ersten Roman beendet, einen düsteren, jedoch humorvollen Krimi.

EINIGE WORTE VORAB…

Sie lesen gerne Krimis und möchten etwas für Ihr Englisch tun? Mit diesen spannenden Kurzkrimis frischen Sie Ihr Englisch auf. Die verwendete Sprache passt genau zum angegebenen Lernniveau von A1-A2, so dass Ihnen das Lesen ganz leicht fällt.

Nicht nur Krimis lesen, sondern auch mehr über Land und Leute erfahren:
Im Anschluss an jede Geschichte finden Sie wissenswerte Informationen zu den **Tatorten und Schauplätzen**, an denen die Geschichten spielen.

Wo die einzelnen Tatorte liegen, können Sie in der **Weltkarte** auf den Seiten 6 und 7 nachschauen.

Schwierigere Wörter sind auf jeder Seite in den **Fußnoten** übersetzt. Im Anhang können Sie nochmals alle Wörter in einer alphabetischen **Wortliste** nachschlagen.

Alle Wörter, die in den Fußnoten übersetzt sind, können Sie mit der **PONS Vokabeltrainer-App** üben. Gehen Sie einfach auf www.pons.de/kurzkrimis-en und laden Sie die App kostenlos auf Ihr Smartphone oder Tablet herunter!

INHALTSVERZEICHNIS

☠ = Geschichte mit extra Gruselfaktor

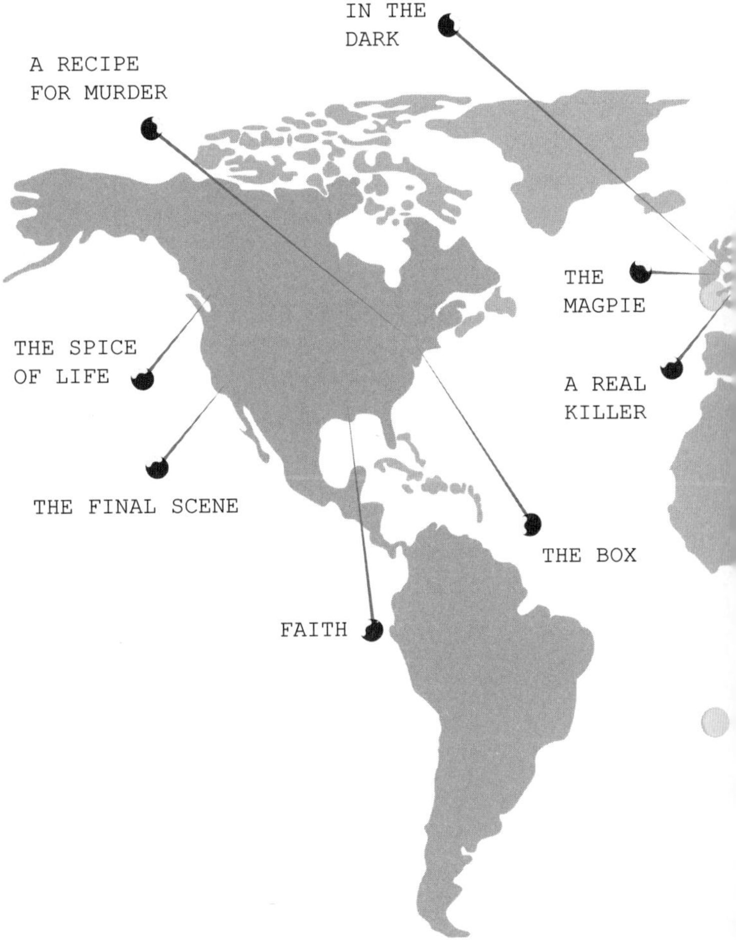
IN THE DARK
A RECIPE FOR MURDER
THE MAGPIE
THE SPICE OF LIFE
A REAL KILLER
THE FINAL SCENE
THE BOX
FAITH

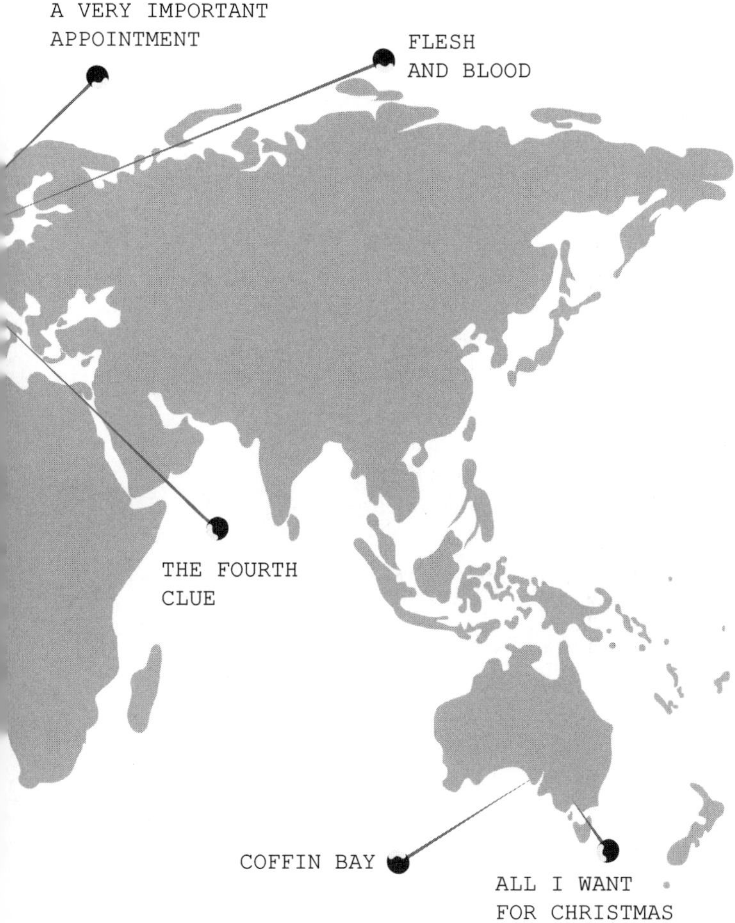
A VERY IMPORTANT APPOINTMENT
FLESH AND BLOOD
THE FOURTH CLUE
COFFIN BAY
ALL I WANT FOR CHRISTMAS

1. A RECIPE FOR MURDER

The noisy kitchen at the back of Rosetta's Bistro is hotter than usual this evening, the last of New York's summer sun adding to the heat from the ovens, making the small space seem like a sauna.

Normally, Ricky Russo, the **head chef**[1], hates the heat; but not tonight.

"I need some air," he shouts to his **sous-chef**[2], Max. "Watch that sauce. Make sure it doesn't burn."

"Yes, chef," says the taller, younger man. "But we're pretty busy here. **Don't be too long**[3]."

Ricky pushes open the back door and steps out into the fresh air of the **alley**[4] in **Hell's Kitchen**[5].

"Don't be too long," he says to himself, angrily. "Who does he think he is?"

He takes his pack of cigarettes from his pocket, pulls one out, and lights it.

For eight years, Ricky Russo has been the head chef at Rosetta's. Most people, however, seem to forget that really the restaurant is his.

Sure, it's his wife's name on the sign outside. And okay, it was her parents who gave him the money to buy the building in the first place.

But who is it that works ten hours every day, every week? Who is it that **sweats and bleeds**[6] and cries for this place?

1 **head chef** - *Chefkoch, Küchenchef(in)*
2 **sous-chef** - *stellvertretende(r) Küchenchef(in), Souschef(in)*
3 **Don't be too long!** - *Brauch nicht zu lang!*
4 **alley** - *Gasse*
5 **Hell's Kitchen** - *Stadtviertel in Manhattan, New York*
6 **to sweat and bleed** - *sich abrackern*

Rosetta? **Yeah right**[1]! All she does is eat the food he cooks and spend the money he makes.

Her parents? All they do is **complain**[2] that the restaurant isn't making enough money, while at the same time bringing their friends here three times a week and drinking as much free wine as possible.

"They think you're an idiot, Ricky," he says, **taking a cloth from his apron**[3] and wiping the sweat from his **bald head**[4]. "They think they can **walk all over**[5] you."

Well, not any more, he thinks, a thin smile appearing on his red face.

Yes, this evening Ricky likes the heat. He likes that everyone in New York is sweating. He likes it because it means that no one notices how nervous he is.

"It has to be tonight, Ricky," he says to himself. "Everything's ready. It's now or never."

He moves back to the door and opens it a little, just enough to be able to see into the kitchen.

Max is shouting orders at the kitchen staff **like he owns the place**[6]. The waiters and waitresses are so busy that they don't have time to think about anything other than which plate is going to which table.

And out in the restaurant, on the best table in the whole place, Rosetta and her parents are waiting for their main course.

"Chef?" Max shouts. "We need a little help in here."

Ricky drops his cigarette, opens the door, and tries **to seem calm**[7]. He hates Max as much as he hates Rosetta and her parents.

"Okay, Max. What's next?"

"We're ready for Rosetta's table."

1 **Yeah right! (ugs.)** – *Ja klar!*
2 **to complain** – *sich beschweren*
3 **to take a cloth from one's apron** – *ein kleines Tuch aus der Schürze nehmen*
4 **bald head** – *Kahlkopf, Glatzkopf*
5 **to walk all over sb.** – *jdn. schikanieren, jdn. ausnutzen*
6 **like sb. owns the place** – *als ob jd. der Besitzer wäre*
7 **to seem calm** – *ruhig erscheinen*

"Easy. Three steaks and **all the trimmings**[1]. The meat's nearly ready. Have you finished those mushrooms? You know they don't like them too cooked." Ricky is so nervous that he nearly laughs, but Max doesn't notice.

This is it. If the sous-chef looks too carefully at those horrible little mushrooms, he might see that something is wrong.

"Come on Max. Get them in the pan."

An angry **expression**[2] appears on the taller man's face, but the sous-chef says nothing. Without a word, he pushes the mushrooms into the hot oil.

Yes, that's right Max. You cook the mushrooms. You always cook the mushrooms; and everyone knows it.

"Two minutes," Max says.

Two minutes. Can it really be this easy?

For the first time in months, Ricky actually starts to think that his plan might work.

But of course it'll work[3]. It's perfect.

Ricky remembers the day he first thought of the idea: Rosetta was in the kitchen talking to Max, smiling at him in that way that Ricky hates. She said that Max should have more responsibilities in the restaurant. She said that Ricky works too hard, that Max could be head chef a couple of nights a week, and that maybe he could be the one who chooses all the food from the market.

It's funny, because that was also the first day that Ricky began to think that Rosetta and Max **were having an affair**[4]. After that, he often saw them talking and smiling at each other. Every time Ricky entered the room, they stopped and looked at him, their expressions **guilty**[5] and their eyes nervous.

"One minute," Max shouts, bringing Ricky back from his memories.

1 **all the trimmings (Pl.)** – *die ganzen Beilagen; alles, was dazugehört*
2 **expression** – *Ausdruck; Miene*
3 **But of course it'll work.** – *Aber natürlich wird das klappen.*
4 **to have an affair** – *eine Affäre haben, fremdgehen*
5 **guilty** – *schuldbewusst*

He takes three plates and places them on the **counter**[1] in front of him. Then, opening the oven, he removes the perfectly cooked steaks and places them on the plates to cool.

Yes, this is it. After three months of thinking about it, this is it.

The only difficult part was replacing the normal mushrooms, the ones that Max bought at the market, with the **extremely poisonous**[2] ones that Ricky bought in the horrible little shop on the other side of the city. **Death Cap mushrooms**[3]; what a fantastic name, Ricky thinks.

"Ready, Chef," Max says, bringing the mushrooms and other vegetables to the counter and placing them carefully onto the plate.

Sure, Ricky thinks, the police are going to ask a lot of questions in the next few weeks. But the plan is so simple that no one will ever be able **to prove**[4] that Ricky **is involved**[5].

Max buys the mushrooms. Max cooks the mushrooms. Max serves the mushrooms.

Of course, he'll probably have to close the restaurant, but **who cares**[6]? When Rosetta and her terrible parents are dead, all of their money will go to Ricky.

Perfect.

"Table five," he shouts, and a waitress runs into the kitchen and picks up the plates.

As he watches her move back into the kitchen, he finally lets himself laugh.

"What's so funny, Chef?" asks Max.

Ricky turns to the other man and smiles. "Oh nothing, nothing. It's just something funny that I thought of." Something like you spending the rest of your life in **jail**[7], he thinks.

1 **counter** - *Theke*
2 **extremely poisonous** - *sehr giftig, hochgiftig*
3 **Death Cap mushroom** - *grüner Knollenblätterpilz*
4 **to prove** - *beweisen*
5 **to be involved** - *beteiligt sein, mit drin stecken*
6 **Who cares?** - *Wen kümmert es?*
7 **jail (AE)** - *Gefängnis*

The other man looks at him for a second, but soon returns to the pasta that he is cooking.

Suddenly, feeling happier than he has in a long time, Ricky opens a bottle of brandy that he keeps in the kitchen for cooking, **pours himself a glass**[1], and starts to drink it.

"Chef," says the same waitress, a few minutes later. "Your wife and her parents would like to see you."

"What?" Ricky asks, the glass of brandy still in his hand.

"They said that it would **only take a minute**[2]."

"Go on, Ricky. I'm okay in here for a moment," says Max.

Suddenly, the head chef of Rosetta's Bistro does not feel so hot any more. In fact, his whole body feels horribly cold. He looks at the waitress, then looks at Max, too. They both have strange expressions on their faces; like they know something that he doesn't.

Jesus. Do they know about the mushrooms? About the plan?

The kitchen seems very quiet now, the restaurant too. It seems like all of the staff are watching him **from the corner of their eyes**[3].

"Go on, Chef," Max says. "You know Rosetta doesn't like **to be kept waiting**[4]."

Slowly, Ricky Russo walks across the kitchen and pushes open the door to the restaurant.

"Surprise!" a hundred familiar voices shout.

"Wh..what?" **he finally manages to**[5] say, looking around at all the people who are smiling at him.

Then Max is behind him, pushing him gently to the table where Rosetta and her parents are waiting for him.

"Happy **anniversary**[6], darling," Rosetta says, putting her arms around him and placing a kiss on his cold cheek.

1 **to pour oneself a glass** - *sich ein Glas einschenken*
2 **to only take a minute** - *nur eine Minute dauern*
3 **from the corner of their eyes** - *aus den Augenwinkeln*
4 **to be kept waiting** - *warten gelassen werden*
5 **to finally manage to do sth.** - *schließlich gelingen, etw. zu tun*
6 **anniversary** - *Jahrestag*

"Anniversary?"

"Yes, don't you remember? It's exactly eight years since we opened the restaurant."

Then Rosetta's father is standing next to him, a large smile on his face. "Well done, Ricky. We all know we don't say it enough, so we wanted to have this little party for you."

Ricky turns around, suddenly realising that he **recognised**[1] every person in the room.

"Max has been helping me **to plan the whole thing**[2]. Isn't that nice of him?" Rosetta continues. "And guess what? Tomorrow we're going on holiday: a three-month cruise! I've been saving a little money every month for the last couple of years."

"You and Max? You mean...? A cruise?"

"And that's not all," said Rosetta's father. "Let's forget about that last bit of money that **you owe us**[3]. I'm going to send the **paperwork**[4] to my **solicitor**[5] tomorrow. When you get back from your holiday, this place is all yours!"

"Really? I can't believe it. I don't know what to say..."

"Oh, you don't need to say anything," said Rosetta's mother, who is still sitting at the table eating. "You just keep cooking excellent food like this. I don't know what your **recipe**[6] is, but these mushrooms are excellent today. This restaurant is going to be **famous**[7]! Absolutely famous!"

And when Ricky Russo looks down at the empty plates on Rosetta's table, the only thing he can do is laugh.

But it is a horrible, **desperate kind of laugh**[8].

"Yes," he says. "Yes, I think that it will be."

1 **to recognise (BE), to recognize -** *erkennen*
2 **to plan the whole thing -** *das Ganze planen*
3 **to owe sb. sth. -** *jdm. etw. schulden*
4 **paperwork -** *Papierkram*
5 **solicitor -** *Rechtsanwalt, -anwältin*
6 **recipe -** *Rezept*
7 **famous -** *berühmt*
8 **desperate kind of laugh -** *verzweifeltes Lachen*

Hell's Kitchen ist ein Stadtviertel im Westen von Manhattan in **New York City**. Früher war das Viertel verrufen, denn es war korrupt und berüchtigt für seine hohe Kriminalitätsrate. Es gehörte zwar zum Big Apple, hinterließ aber einen bitteren Nachgeschmack, denn nur wenige trauten sich in die Gegend, außer, sie kannten sich dort gut aus.

In den letzten Jahren hat sich der Ruf von Hell's Kitchen gebessert. Die Kriminalitätsrate sank und im Gegenzug stieg das soziale Ansehen des Viertels deutlich. Es ist bei Schauspielern und Künstlern sehr beliebt, und durch seine soziale Aufwertung ziehen mittlerweile auch Geschäftsinhaber und Finanziers der Wall Street dorthin.

Trotz all dieser Veränderungen lauert die kriminelle Vergangenheit noch in den dunklen Gassen, und die Erinnerung an die Verbrechen von damals ist in den Köpfen der Menschen noch immer gegenwärtig.

2. A VERY IMPORTANT APPOINTMENT

The small blue car moves slowly along St Stephen's Street, passes the famous church on its right, and finally parks next to the **row**[1] of tall, **Georgian**[2] houses.

Edinburgh is quiet today, and the cold winter rain makes the **ancient**[3] city seem strangely dark and **sinister**[4].

Inside the car, Detective Munro turns off the engine, looks out of the window, but does not open the door. Instead, she takes a cigarette from her purse and holds it in her right hand. She does not light the cigarette, but **every now and again**[5] she puts it to her mouth and **pretends**[6] to smoke it.

After a few minutes, she puts the cigarette away, looks at herself in the car mirror, then opens the door.

The rain outside is so heavy that as she runs to the red door of the nearest Georgian house, her long dark hair **is soaked**[7]. She pulls the **collar**[8] of her coat up to her face and knocks loudly on the door. Almost immediately, the door opens, and a **well-dressed**[9] gentleman with a silver **beard**[10] smiles at her. "Come in, Detective." "Please, call me Sarah, Professor," she says, and moves into the hallway.

The gentleman smiles. "Let me take your coat."

Sarah takes off her coat and passes it to the older man. "It's very good of you to see me."

1 **row** - *Reihe*
2 **Georgian** - *georgianisch*
3 **ancient** - *(hier) alt*
4 **sinister** - *düster, finster*
5 **every now and again** - *ab und zu*
6 **to pretend to do sth.** - *so tun als ob man etw. tut, vorgeben etw. zu tun*
7 **to be soaked** - *patschnass sein*
8 **collar** - *Kragen*
9 **well-dressed** - *gut gekleidet*
10 **beard** - *Bart*

"I'm always very happy to help the police. Perhaps we can talk in my **study**[1]."

With another smile, the professor turns, walks along the hallway, and opens the door to his study.

It is a medium-sized room, with a large writing desk, three or four bookcases, two long leather sofas, a small coffee table, and several other pieces of elegant furniture.

"Can I offer you a drink, Sarah? Are you allowed to drink when you're working?"

"Well, actually, I'm not working today. Like I told you on the phone, I wanted to speak to you about some **research**[2] that I'm doing. It's not official police business at the moment."

"Then perhaps I can offer you a whisky? It might make you feel a little warmer on this horrible winter day."

"That would be nice, thank you."

The professor moves to a small table, opens a bottle of whisky, and **pours**[3] two glasses of Scotch. "**Make yourself comfortable**[4]," he says, and passes her a glass.

Then, with another smile, he sits down on the sofa opposite her. "What can I help you with?"

"Do you know what a **cold case**[5] is, professor?"

"No, I don't think that I do."

"Well, a cold case is when the police have tried **to solve a crime**[6], but they don't have enough **evidence**[7] to find a **culprit**[8]."

"I understand."

"A few months ago, I found one of these cold cases that I thought was extremely interesting."

"Really?"

1 **study** - *Arbeitszimmer*
2 **research** - *Recherche, Recherchearbeit*
3 **to pour sth.** - *etw. einschenken*
4 **to make oneself comfortable** - *es sich bequem machen*
5 **cold case** - *ungeklärter Kriminalfall*
6 **to solve a crime** - *einen Fall lösen*
7 **evidence** - *Beweis*
8 **culprit** - *Täter(in)*

"Yes. **Unfortunately**[1], my boss doesn't agree with me. He thinks we have enough problems here in Edinburgh already."

The professor laughs. "I think he might be correct. Are you allowed to tell me about the case?"

"Not the details, but I can tell you some of the more general information." Sarah tastes her own whisky, places the glass on the table, and begins. "Two years ago, a young woman from Edinburgh was found dead in the **forest**[2] near Blackford Hill. Do you remember?"

"Yes, I think I do," says the professor. "The woman's **throat**[3] was cut, but her killer was never found."

"That's right. It was strange because her friends and family couldn't tell us why she was in the forest. Well, a few months ago, while I was looking at cold cases, I found another **similar**[4] murder. Four years ago, another young woman was found dead in the trees at Abercorn Park."

The professor nods. "And this woman was killed in the same way? Her throat was cut?"

"No, she **was strangled**[5]. However, I noticed in the report that her friends and family also thought it was strange that she was in the park. She didn't live in that area. There was no reason for her to be there."

"Well, I'm not sure I see the **connection**[6]."

Sarah laughs. "Exactly what my boss said. But there was something similar about the case. The women were the same age, they looked similar, they were in places where they normally never went. So I started to look at other cases."

"And did you find anything?"

1 **unfortunately** - *leider*
2 **forest** - *Wald*
3 **throat** - *Kehle*
4 **similar** - *ähnlich*
5 **to be strangled** - *erdrosselt werden*
6 **connection** - *Verbindung*

Sarah reaches into her bag and pulls out a large **folder**[1]. "Yes, I found eight similar cases. In each case a young woman was found in a quiet park or forest, not far from Edinburgh. Each of them was killed in a different way, but there was always this strange fact that they normally never went to these places."

The professor puts his glass down on the table and **leans forward**[2]. "Yes, I can see now why you think this is interesting. So how can I help you? Would you like me to **suggest**[3] the kind of person who might **commit**[4] a crime like this?"

"Oh no, that's not really why I'm here. I know that you're a professor of psychology, and that you could explain the mind of the killer to me, but I have another reason for coming here."

The professor pauses. "Really?"

"Yes, you see, a few months ago, I decided to **quit**[5] smoking. A friend of mine suggested that I should try hypnosis. It was excellent. The doctor helped me to completely stop."

"Well, that is good news, but I don't see the connection with the cases."

"Well, it was while I was having hypnosis that I remembered something."

"And what was that?"

"On the day the women died, each one of them stopped what they were doing. They turned to a friend or colleague, and said that they had an important **appointment**[6] that they must go to."

"I'm not sure that I understand. Lots of people have appointments that they forget."

1 **folder -** *Aktenordner*
2 **to lean forward -** *sich nach vorne lehnen*
3 **to suggest sth. -** *etw. vorschlagen*
4 **to commit sth. -** *etw. begehen*
5 **to quit -** *aufhören*
6 **appointment -** *Verabredung, Termin*

"Yes, but professor, each woman said exactly the same thing. *I'm very sorry but I have to go; I have a very important appointment.* Those are the last words that each of these eight women said. Don't you think that it's strange?"

The older man sits back in his seat, his glass of whisky in his hand. "I think that I'm beginning to understand. You think that each of those poor women **were hypnotised**[1]."

"Exactly. I asked my doctor about it, but he said he didn't think that it was possible. He said that it is very difficult to make someone do what they don't want to do."

"Your doctor is correct. I know a little bit about hypnotism and I completely agree."

"A little bit? Professor, I think that you're being **modest**[2]. A lot of people have told me that you know more about **hypnotism**[3] than anyone else in Edinburgh. That's why I'm here."

The professor pauses again. "You want me to tell you about hypnotism?"

"No," says Sarah. "I want you to **hypnotise**[4] me. I want to know if it's possible for you to make me do something that I don't want to do."

For a moment the professor says nothing, but he looks at Sarah with an **unreadable expression**[5] in his eyes.

"Does that sound **mad**[6]?" Sarah asks, and laughs again.

"Well, it is a little bit strange, but I think that it might help you to understand that your doctor is correct."

"So you'll try?"

Again, the professor pauses. "Yes, of course. Anything to help the police. It's actually very easy to hypnotise someone if

1 **to be hypnotised (BE), to be hypnotized -** *hypnotisiert werden*
2 **modest -** *bescheiden*
3 **hypnotism -** *Kunst der Hypnose*
4 **to hypnotise (BE) sb., to hypnotize sb. -** *jdn. hypnotisieren, jdn. in Hypnose versetzen*
5 **unreadable expression -** *(Gesichts)ausdruck, der sich nicht deuten lässt*
6 **mad -** *verrückt*

they have been hypnotised before. All you have to do is relax. Can you do that for me, Sarah? Lean back in your seat and relax."

"Okay," says Sarah, a nervous smile on her face.

"Close your eyes. Listen only to the sound of my voice. You're very safe here, Sarah. You're very safe and you're very relaxed. Close your eyes and **breathe**[1] slowly."

Sarah begins to lean back into the sofa, and her eyes slowly start to close.

"That's good, Sarah. That's excellent. Now, listen only to the sound of my voice. Your body feels very relaxed now. You feel very safe. Repeat what I say, Sarah. I feel very relaxed. I feel very safe."

In a strange and slow **tone of voice**[2], Sarah repeats the words. "I feel very relaxed. I feel very safe."

"Excellent," says the professor. "Now, Sarah, I want you to answer my questions, but when we finish, I don't want you to remember anything. Do you understand?"

"I understand," says Sarah, in the same strange voice.

"Does anybody know that you're here today, Sarah?"

"No."

"Did you tell your boss that you were going to speak to me about hypnotism?"

"No."

"Did anybody see you enter my house?"

"No."

"Good. Now, Sarah, tell me, do you know who killed those women?"

For a moment, Sarah does not reply.

"Sarah?"

"No," she says, her eyes still closed, her body now completely relaxed.

1 **to breathe** - *atmen, einatmen*
2 **tone of voice** - *Tonfall*

"Excellent," says the professor, and a **contented smile**[1] appears on his face. "Now, Sarah, I want you to listen to me very carefully: Tomorrow, at exactly four o'clock in the afternoon, I want you to stop whatever you're doing, and go to Saughton Park. Don't tell anyone where you are going, Sarah. If anyone asks… just say that you have a very important appointment."

St Stephen's Street liegt in Stockbridge, einem eleganten, historischen Stadtviertel der Stadt **Edinburgh** in Schottland. Die berühmte Kirche von St Stephen's sowie die georgianische Architektur der Wohnhäuser führen zur Beliebtheit des Viertels bei reichen Akademikern, Geschäftsleuten und sogar bei Prominenten.

Da das Viertel in der Nähe von grünen Parkanlagen und luxuriösen Geschäften liegt, verschlägt es Touristen und Einwohner gleichermaßen gerne dorthin. Es gibt dort auch exquisite Antiquitätenläden, Cafés und Kunstgalerien.

Bei Regen oder an dunklen Wintertagen scheint aber sogar über diesem attraktiven Stadtteil ein dunkler Schatten von Verbrechen und Geheimnissen zu liegen.

1 **contented smile** - *zufriedenes Lächeln*

3. A REAL KILLER

Frank likes the way that the **changing room**[1] becomes silent as he begins to remove his shirt.

There are only a few other men here at this time of the evening, but they all quickly move their eyes away from the **scarred and tattooed body**[2] of the large, **intimidating**[3] man in front of them.

In his early fifties now, Frank knows that he is not at his peak of physical fitness any more. His shoulders and arms are still impressively **muscled**[4], but his stomach is too large and his fat **spills out**[5] over the white towel that he wears around his **waist**[6].

But Frank doesn't care. No, he might not be twenty-one any more, but his scars and tattoos are terrifying enough to let anyone know what sort of man Frank Cole is; a dangerous criminal.

"Have a good evening, Mr Cole," one man says, as he quickly leaves the changing room.

At the sound of his name, the other men seem to become even more nervous.

With a **cruel**[7] smile that reveals his two gold teeth, Frank watches them hurry from the small changing room, happy at the effect of his dangerous **reputation**[8].

1 **changing room** - *Umkleidekabine; Umkleideraum*
2 **scarred and tattooed body** - *vernarbter und mit Tätowierungen übersäter Körper*
3 **intimidating** - *angsteinflößend*
4 **muscled** - *muskulös*
5 **to spill out** - *(hier) (heraus)quellen*
6 **waist** - *Taille*
7 **cruel** - *grausam*
8 **reputation** - *Ruf*

Alone now, he closes his **locker**[1] and walks into the large main room of the bathhouse. It is a beautiful old building, blue and white **tiles**[2] on the high walls, a deep central pool filled with crystal clear water, and four gold **fountains**[3] in the corners of the room.

And it is all his. Just one of the many properties that he owns in the East End of London.

He starts to walk towards the sauna at the far end of the room, happy that the bathhouse is now empty.

"You're too late," a voice says. "We're closing."

Frank turns and sees an **elderly cleaner**[4] in a uniform.

"Mr Cole? I'm sorry, Sir, I didn't recognise you. I…"

Frank holds up his finger and **silences**[5] the old man. "It's fine, Ben," he says, reading the **nametag**[6] on the man's uniform. "Are you new here?"

The old man shakes his head. "I've been here for more than a year, but I normally work in the mornings, Sir."

Frank nods. "You can go. I'll **lock up**[7] when **I'm done**[8]."

Without another word, Frank turns and continues to move towards the sauna.

When he reaches the door, he opens it and enjoys the feeling of the **heat**[9] on his body. He is about to enter when he hears a noise behind him.

"I said you could go," he says.

Then the pain explodes on the back of his neck and he falls forwards. Before he can stop himself, his head **strikes**[10] the **marble bench**[11] inside the sauna, and darkness fills his mind.

"Mr Cole?" a gentle voice says. "Can you hear me, Mr Cole?"

1 **locker** - *Schließfach, Spind*
2 **tile** - *Fliese*
3 **fountain** - *Springbrunnen*
4 **elderly cleaner** - *ältere Reinigungskraft*
5 **to silence sb.** - *jdn. zum Schweigen bringen*
6 **nametag** - *Namensschild*
7 **to lock up** - *abschließen*
8 **to be done** - *fertig sein*
9 **heat** - *Hitze*
10 **to strike** - *(hier) aufschlagen*
11 **marble bench** - *Marmorbank*

On the floor of the sauna, his body **covered in sweat**[1], Frank **struggles**[2] to open his eyes. “What happened?” he asks, his thoughts confused.

“You fell,” says the voice. “You hit your head. I was worried about you.” The voice sounds strange, like it is far away.

“I fell?” Frank asks.

Then he feels the pain at the back of his neck and he remembers.

“Someone hit me,” he says. “I’ll kill them, I’ll…”

Then he hears a slow, dangerous laugh, and Frank’s eyes **snap open**[3]. “Who are you?” he says as he slowly **manages to stand**[4].

A face appears at the small window in the door of the sauna.

“You?” Frank says, when he sees the face of the elderly cleaner. He tries to open the door, but the handle doesn’t turn. “Let me out of here, old man.”

The cleaner smiles. “Frank Cole. The big boss. Thinks he can tell everyone what to do. It is hot enough for you in there, Mr Cole? I hope so.”

Frank **bangs his fists against**[5] the door. “Let me out of here.”

The cleaner shakes his head. “No. I don’t think that I will.”

Frank screams in anger and hits the door again and again.

“It won’t work, Mr Cole. This is a strong door. Strong glass too. Almost **unbreakable**[6]. Why don’t you sit down? Relax. That’s why you come here every Friday, isn’t it? To relax.”

Frank stops hitting the door, but the anger doesn’t leave his face.

“What are you going to do?” he says. “What next?”

“Nothing. All we do is wait,” and his voice is so calm that it **sends a shiver down Frank’s spine**[7].

1 **covered in sweat** – *schweißbedeckt*
2 **to struggle to do sth.** – *sich schwertun etw. zu tun; damit kämpfen etw. zu tun*
3 **to snap open** – *aufschlagen*
4 **to manage to stand** – *es schaffen zu stehen*
5 **to bang one’s fists against sth.** – *mit den Fäusten gegen etw. schlagen*
6 **unbreakable** – *unzerbrechlich*
7 **to send a shiver down one’s spine** – *jdm. einen Schauer über den Rücken jagen*

"Who are you?" asks Frank.

"Nobody, Frank. I'm nobody. But I was someone's father… once. A long time ago."

Frank feels the sweat begin to fall from his head and chest. "So that's it, is it?" he says, and he **forces**[1] another cruel smile. "Someone killed your kid?"

For the first time, the old man hesitates. "Yes, his name was David. David Riggs."

Frank laughs. "You stupid idiot. I've never heard of him. You've just made the biggest mistake of your life." Frank sits down on the marble bench and watches the face in the window. "Oh, Ben, Ben, Ben. What have you done? I don't know who killed your boy, but it wasn't me."

In the window, a dark expression crossed the face of the old cleaner. "You killed him, Frank. You and those drugs you sell."

"Drugs?" Frank shouts, as he **wipes**[2] the sweat from his eyes. "I don't sell drugs. I sell property, you idiot."

"Oh yes, Frank the businessman. Do you really think anyone believes that? No, you're the same dirty little criminal that you always have been."

"You can't speak to me like that!" Frank says as he stands up. Then he runs at the door and hits it with his shoulder.

When the door moves, Frank **grins**[3] and strikes it again and again, and his huge body makes the whole wall **shake**[4].

Finally, after more than five minutes, he falls back onto the marble bench, his face bright red, and his body **soaked in sweat**[5].

"Is that it, Mr Cole? Is that all you have?"

"I'll kill you," Frank **gasps**[6].

"No, I don't think so. You see, you're not a real killer. A real killer is patient and calm. A real killer follows his victims

1 **to force sth.** - *etw. erzwingen*
2 **to wipe** - *wischen*
3 **to grin** - *grinsen*
4 **to shake** - *(hier) beben*
5 **soaked in sweat** - *schweißgebadet*
6 **to gasp** - *keuchen*

and watches them. People are **creatures of habit**[1], Frank. A real killer learns the habits of their **prey**[2]. I've followed you for nearly ten years; watching you, learning about you. That's what a real killer does."

"Ten years? You **pathetic**[3] little man. Your boy died ten years ago, and you didn't do anything!"

"I had the opportunity to kill you many times. I stood behind you, a knife or rope in my hand. But that's not the way you **deserve to die**[4]."

"Pathetic. And even when you have me on the floor you can't do it. You know what? I don't think you can do it now."

At the window, the face of the cleaner doesn't move.

Frank laughs and looks around the room, thinking for the first time. The other **employees**[5] will be back in the morning. They open at eight o'clock seven days a week. Does the old man have a gun on the other side of the door? Frank isn't sure, but he doesn't think so.

Then, in the corner of the sauna, he sees a brown **bucket**[6] half full of water. "You idiot," Frank laughs again. "You talk about being a real killer, but you don't even check to see if there's any water in here?" He moves to the bucket and picks it up. There must be about a litre of water. If the old man doesn't open the door, he can use the water to survive until the morning. If the old man does open the door… well, then Frank Cole will show the idiot exactly what a real killer is **capable of**[7].

With the cleaner still watching his every move, Frank lifts the bucket to his lips and drinks. The water is almost as hot as the room, and the taste is strangely sweet, but it will be enough to keep him alive.

1 **creatures of habit (Pl.)** - *Gewohnheitstiere*
2 **prey** - *Beute*
3 **pathetic** - *armselig, erbärmlich*
4 **to deserve to die** - *es verdienen zu sterben*
5 **employee** - *Angestellte(r)*
6 **bucket** - *Eimer*
7 **to be capable of sth.** - *zu etw. im Stande sein*

At the window, the old man speaks again. "Do you know how my boy died? Do you know what those horrible drugs did to him?"

Frank takes another drink and sits down on the marble bench again. "I don't care, old man."

"It was the heat, they told me. The drugs made his heart beat faster, raised his **blood pressure**[1], made him lose control of himself. But it was the heat that killed him." The old man stops speaking and looks at the thermometers on the wall of the sauna. "How hot it is in there, Mr Cole? It must be painful now. Soon you'll start to **feel dizzy**[2], then you'll **pass out**[3]."

Frank laughs again. "You really are an idiot. Look at me. Look at my body. I've been shot twice, **stabbed a dozen times**[4]. I've been in more fights than I can remember. Do you really think that I can't survive a night in this heat? Do you really think that this is going to kill me?" And Frank takes another drink of water from the bucket.

For a moment, the old man says nothing. His face is dark and serious, and Frank even thinks that he sees an **expression of sadness**[5] in the man's eyes.

"No," the old man finally **replies**[6]. "But the drugs that I put in that water will."

"What?" asks Frank, the smile still on his face.

"The same drugs that killed my boy, but a hundred times stronger. You've drunk enough now. A mouthful is enough to kill ten men your size. Can you feel it? Is your heart starting to beat faster? My boy died alone in the corner of some horrible night club. But don't worry… Frank. You won't die alone. I'm not going anywhere."

1 **blood pressure** – *Blutdruck*
2 **to feel dizzy** – *sich schwindelig fühlen*
3 **to pass out** – *ohnmächtig werden*
4 **to have been stabbed a dozen times** – *mehrere Dutzend Stichwunden erlitten haben*
5 **expression of sadness** – *trauriger Ausdruck*
6 **to reply** – *antworten*

And Frank is about to laugh at the old man, but then he feels something strange in his chest. And **instead**[1], when he opens his mouth, it is a terrified and painful scream that fills the sauna.

But there is no one to hear it, **apart from**[2] the old cleaner.

Viele Jahre lang galt das **Londoner East End** als eines der gefährlichsten Viertel der berühmten Hauptstadt Englands. Die Kriminalitätsrate war sehr hoch, nicht zuletzt aufgrund der vielen sozialen Probleme und der hohen Armutsrate des Viertels. In den 1960er Jahren beherrschten Gangster die Gegend wie z. B. die berüchtigten Kray-Zwillinge.

Zwanzig Jahre später, in den 80er Jahren, veränderte sich das Viertel durch die Schließung der *Docklands* (Hafenviertel). Allerdings blieben einige charakteristische Gebäude bestehen, zum Beispiel die luxuriösen türkischen oder russischen Badehäuser, von denen einige bereits aus dem späten 19. Jahrhundert stammten. Der schottische Diplomat und Politiker David Urquhart hatte die Tradition der Badehäuser auf seinen Reisen nach Konstantinopel entdeckt und nach Großbritannien importiert. Unter seiner Aufsicht eröffnete 1862 das erste türkische Hammam in der Jermyn Street. Bis weit ins 20. Jahrhundert hinein waren Badehäuser nur für Männer zugänglich und beliebte Treffpunkte für Geschäftsleute, Stadträte und schließlich auch für die kriminelle Unterwelt.

1 **instead** – *stattdessen*
2 **apart from** – *abgesehen von*

4. THE FINAL SCENE

"Good evening, gentlemen. Mr Von Schmidt has asked me to show you to the veranda," says the tall, **wide-shouldered**[1] butler with cold, dead eyes.

Private detectives James White and Terrence Cole step into the entrance of the mansion and look around. They are both of average height, dressed in long raincoats, with dark hair and darker eyes. The only real difference between the two men is the fact that Cole's face seems to like smiling, while White's is serious and **difficult to read**[2].

"This is an impressive old building," says Cole.

The butler says nothing, but turns and begins to walk across the elegant **foyer**[3].

"Who is this guy, Frankenstein's monster?" Cole **mutters**[4].

White says nothing, and the two men follow the silent butler.

"Our normal clients don't live in places like this, White."

White **nods**[5] his head. "Yeah, which is why we never get paid any real money," he says quietly. "This guy lives in the Hollywood Hills. That means money."

"The veranda," the butler says, opening a door at the end of a long hallway.

The two men step out onto a wide **wooden terrace**[6]. To their right, they can see the large white letters of the Hollywood sign.

1 **wide-shouldered -** *breitschultrig*
2 **to be difficult to read -** *(hier) schwer zu deuten sein*
3 **foyer -** *Empfangshalle*
4 **to mutter -** *murmeln*
5 **to nod -** *nicken*
6 **wooden terrace -** *Holzterrasse*

To their left, the city of Los Angeles **twinkles**[1] with a million lights in the darkness.

"Wow. Now that is what I call a view," Cole laughs.

"I'm happy that you like it," says a voice, and they turn to see a very old man, who is watching them from his **wheelchair**[2].

"Mr Von Schmidt, these are detectives Cole and White," says the butler.

"Thank you, Harold." The old man moves his wheelchair forwards. "I'm very happy to see you, gentlemen. Could I offer you anything to drink?"

"I think it's better if we know why we're here first, Mr Von Schmidt," says White. "Your butler didn't explain very much on the phone."

"Yes. Harold is very useful, but he is a simple man. Loyal, strong, but simple." The old man looks at the butler and smiles kindly. "But let me ask you something first, gentlemen; do you know who I am?"

The two detectives **shake their heads**[3]. "Sorry, but no. Should we?" says Cole.

"No. Not anymore. **However**[4], there was a time when everyone in this city knew my name."

"Were you an actor?" White asks, as he takes a cigarette from his pocket and lights it.

"No, a film director."

"Really? What type of films?"

"Oh, many different genres, Mr Cole. But perhaps I was most famous for my horrors. I was one of the first to **experiment**[5] with what you now call special effects. I created monsters and demons from plastic and wax, and I won many **awards**[6]."

1 **to twinkle** - *glitzern*
2 **wheelchair** - *Rollstuhl*
3 **to shake one's head** - *den Kopf schütteln*
4 **however** - *aber, jedoch*
5 **to experiment** - *experimentieren*
6 **award** - *Preis*

"Really? It's strange that we've never heard your name before," says White.

"No, it's not strange, Mr White. Hollywood can be **cruel**[1]. If this place wants people to forget you, then people will forget you."

"And why did it want people to forget you, Mr Von Schmidt?" asks Cole.

"A scandal. A terrible scandal. I married an actress, a beautiful young woman called Sylvia Sinclair. She was the love of my life, but I was a fool. I thought that I needed more than just her. I thought that I was so important that I **deserved**[2] more than her."

"You **had an affair**[3]?" asks White.

An **expression of pain**[4] moves across the old director's face. "I had… many affairs. Many. It is the biggest **regret**[5] of my life."

Cole shakes his head. "Hollywood loves affairs. They love the drama. They don't make people forget about famous directors because of them."

"You're right. But one night something terrible happened. It was here, in this house, nearly fifty years ago, that my wife was killed." The old man lifts his hand and points to another door at the far side of the veranda. "There, in my wife's music room. That is where it happened. Someone entered that room and **stabbed her in the chest**[6]."

The two detectives look at the door, then **exchange doubtful glances**[7]. "But, Mr Von Schmidt, if that was fifty years ago, why are we here now?"

1 **cruel** - *grausam*
2 **to deserve sb.** - *jdn. verdienen*
3 **to have an affair** - *eine Affäre haben*
4 **expression of pain** - *schmerzhafter Ausdruck*
5 **regret** - *Reue, Bedauern*
6 **to stab sb. in the chest** - *jdn. in die Brust stechen*
7 **to exchange doubtful glances** - *skeptische Blicke austauschen*

"Because the police never did their job," says Von Schmidt, his voice suddenly angry. "They decided that my wife… my poor, sweet wife, had **killed herself**[1]."

"And Hollywood believed them," says White, quietly.

"It was the end of my career. The end of my… everything. My family, my friends, they all thought it was my fault. Only poor Harold stayed loyal to me." The old man turns his chair back to them. "But I knew Sylvia. It was no **suicide**[2]. Somebody entered that room and killed her. I don't know who. **I don't care**[3] who. I only want people to know that it was not suicide. And that is why you are here."

White shakes his head. "Why now?"

The old man laughs. "Look at me, Mr White. I'm not a **healthy**[4] man. Harold does everything for me now. He is my arms and legs. Before I die, I must show the people the **truth**[5]. I would do anything for them to know that it was not suicide. Anything."

Cole moves to stand beside his partner. "So what do you want us to do? Look at the notes from the case?"

"Oh no, Mr Cole. No, I want you **to investigate**[6] the **scene of the crime**[7]."

For a moment neither detective says anything.

The old man smiles. "You see, in the last few months, I **have recreated**[8] the final scene from that terrible night. There were many police pictures. Hundreds. Carefully, Harold and I have used them to create a **perfect representation**[9] of Sylvia's murder. All I ask, is that you enter the room and give me your professional opinion."

1 **to kill oneself** - *sich (selbst) umbringen*
2 **suicide** - *Selbstmord*
3 **I don't care** - *Es ist mir egal, …*
4 **healthy** - *gesund*
5 **truth** - *Wahrheit*
6 **to investigate** - *untersuchen*
7 **scene of the crime** - *Tatort*
8 **to recreate sth.** - *etw. nachstellen*
9 **perfect representation** - *exakte Wiedergabe*

White finishes his cigarette and drops it on the veranda. "I don't think we can help, Mr Von Schmidt."

"Harold," the old man signals and the butler moves forwards and takes four envelopes from his jacket pocket.

"Inside the first two envelopes there is ten thousand dollars... each. If you enter the room and examine the scene, that money is yours. However, if you can **prove**[1] that Sylvia's death was not a suicide, you can also take the third and fourth envelopes; both of which contain two hundred thousand dollars."

Cole and White say nothing for a moment, and a **warm breeze**[2] moves across the veranda.

"Well, gentlemen?"

"Well, we can't promise anything," begins White.

"But we can **certainly**[3] look," Cole adds with a smile.

"Excellent. Harold, please go and... prepare the room," he says, his eyes never leaving the face of his butler. "Make sure that everything is perfect."

The butler looks at the old man for a moment then walks to the door, unlocks it, and enters.

"Oh, and gentleman," says Von Schmidt as they move slowly towards the door. "Please don't **be alarmed**[4] by the **mannequin**[5]. I used my knowledge of special effects to create a perfect representation of my poor wife at the time of her death. The figure is the same height, shape and weight. I thought that it might be important for your examination, but the **result**[6] is... well, quite realistic."

Then the door opens once again and the butler stands to one side and holds it open for the two detectives.

"Are you not coming in?" asks White.

1 **to prove** - *beweisen*
2 **warm breeze** - *warmer Lufthauch*
3 **certainly** - *sicherlich*
4 **to be alarmed** - *erschrocken sein*
5 **mannequin** - *Schaufensterpuppe*
6 **result** - *Ergebnis*

"Not yet. First, I would like you to see the room alone. I want you to see it exactly how it was on that terrible night."

"**After you**[1]," says Cole with another smile; and White steps into the room, his partner just behind him.

The room is darker than the veranda, large curtains in front of the window keep out the light from the city, and only one small lamp offers any other **illumination**[2]. It is not a large room, but it is just as elegant as the other parts of the house. In one corner, there is a piano, in another, an old gramophone, boxes of records, and many other musical instruments.

But it is not these things that the two detectives look at. Instead, they move slowly towards the mannequin of a slim, blonde woman, which is lying on its back in the center of the room, blood **slowly spilling**[3] from a **stab wound**[4] in its chest.

"Jesus. It looks so real," says Cole, who covers his mouth with his hands. "Are you sure...?"

For a moment neither man moves, then White walks slowly to the other side of the figure and **kneels down**[5]. "It's not all realistic. Look. Just movie magic."

Cole moves to stand next to his partner and looks down at the strange mannequin. **Instead**[6] of the eyes, nose and mouth, there is only a **smooth plastic mask**[7].

"No face," White says.

"I **guess**[8] the old man didn't want to see it," says Cole quietly.

"Jesus. Why would he do this? Does he really think we can help? What do you think we should do?"

"Stay in here for fifteen minutes, then go and get our money," Cole says, his usual smile now gone.

1 **After you!** - *Nach Ihnen!*
2 **illumination** - *Beleuchtung; Lichtquelle*
3 **to slowly spill** - *langsam herausfließen*
4 **stab wound** - *Stichwunde*
5 **to kneel down** - *sich niederknien*
6 **instead of** - *statt, anstelle von*
7 **smooth plastic mask** - *weiche Plastikmaske*
8 **to guess** - *vermuten, schätzen*

White looks at the strange plastic face again. "But if the old man really recreated the scene of the crime..."

"What? You think we can prove it wasn't suicide? You're crazy."

White stands up and looks around the room. "There is something strange here. I've seen a few suicides, but I've never seen anyone **choose to do**[1] it like this."

"People do crazy things," Cole says, and moves as far from the mannequin as he can.

"And the violin?"

Cole looks at the instrument that is lying next to the body. "It looks like she dropped it there."

"So one moment she was playing the violin, the next she takes a knife, stabs her own chest?"

"And where is the knife?"

"There, next to the sofa."

Cole walks to the window and shakes his head. "Too far from the body."

"Jesus. Were the police really this stupid in the 50s?"

"Maybe there were no **fingerprints**[2], no **evidence**[3] of anyone being in here. If nothing was stolen, then there was no motive."

"So either the **cops**[4] were stupid or lazy?"

White says nothing for a moment. "There is another possibility. We don't know if any of this is real. Why should we believe Von Schmidt? We need to see the pictures of the crime scene before we can make any real decisions."

"Then you will see them, gentlemen," says Von Schmidt. The director and the butler are now standing in the doorway, and there is a smile on the old man's face. "But I knew that this would help you to see the truth. I knew it!"

1 **to choose to do sth.** - *etw. freiwillig tun*
2 **fingerprint** - *Fingerabdruck*
3 **evidence** - *Beweis*
4 **cops (Pl., ugs.)** - *Bullen, Cops*

"Okay, Mr Von Schmidt," White says, as he walks back to the door. "We **agree**[1] that there's something strange here. But we still need more than this. We need to see the pictures of the crime scene, the notes from the case."

"**Of course**[2], of course!" says the old man. "Harold will bring you everything you need. But this is just the beginning, gentlemen. I know it. I know that you can finally help me to find the truth."

"Like I said before, we can't promise anything," says White.

"But we can certainly…" Cole begins to say.

"What?" asks White.

Cole turns back to the room. "Oh, nothing. I thought I heard something."

"Gentlemen, come with me. Your money is waiting. We can examine the case notes in my study."

White looks at the old man and sees a suddenly nervous expression on his face. "What's wrong?"

"Nothing, but we should..."

But before he can finish, a strange noise fills the room.

"Jesus," says Cole. "What is that?"

White turns and moves back towards his partner. "I don't know, music? Singing?"

"No," says Cole.

"It sounds like it's coming from the middle of the room. It sounds like…"

The two men stop, their eyes move towards the mannequin, and **horrified expressions**[3] slowly begin to appear on their faces.

"No. God no. What have you done?" Cole asks.

And from the doorway the old director speaks again. "We had to. You understand, don't you? It had to be realistic. We had

1 **to agree** – *sich einig sein; einwilligen, zustimmen*
2 **of course!** – *natürlich*
3 **horrified expression** – *entsetzter Gesichtsausdruck*

to make you see the truth. But the drugs **were supposed to**[1] **last longer**[2]. We never wanted the poor girl to feel any pain."

But the two detectives are not listening to the old man. They cannot. All they can do is stare at the mannequin and listen to the terrible sound.

The sound coming from behind the plastic mask.

The sound of someone crying.

Die **Hollywood Hills** gehören heute zu den berühmtesten und beliebtesten Gegenden von **Los Angeles**. Hier begann ab etwa 1910 das Filmgewerbe zu florieren und schließlich wurde das riesige Schild, das eigentlich das Wohngebiet Hollywoodland bezeichnete, von der Filmindustrie vereinnahmt. Heute thront in riesigen Lettern der 14 Meter hohe und fast 140 Meter breite HOLLYWOOD-Schriftzug in den Hills und ist zum Wahrzeichen der amerikanischen Filmbranche geworden.

Inzwischen setzt sich die Gegend aus verschiedenen Wohnvierteln zusammen, aber nur wer wirklich Geld hat, kann es sich leisten hier zu leben. Jedoch hört man immer wieder Geschichten von merkwürdigen oder ungelösten Verbrechen, die sich in diesem Teil LAs abgespielt haben sollen.

1 **to be supposed to do sth. –** *etw. angeblich tun sollen*
2 **to last longer –** *länger anhalten (Wirkung)*

5. THE SPICE OF LIFE

I hear the question, but for a moment I don't reply. Instead, I let my eyes move across the view that **rolls past**[1] the window of the long-distance, luxury train.

Canada, such a beautiful, lonely type of country. There are more wide open spaces here than anywhere else that I have ever been. More **emptiness and nothingness**[2]. I both love and hate it. I want to stay forever and escape as quickly as possible. But that's me, I never really know what I want in life.

The sun is high now. The long summer afternoon is slowly moving towards evening. Soon, we'll be in Jasper. Maybe I'll leave the train there, or maybe I'll stay on until Vancouver. From the city, I could travel up the coast to British Colombia, where the real empty places are. **Avoid**[3] other people. Take the time to learn a little more about myself.

I smile at the **thought**[4], then turn away from the mountains and the sunshine, and look instead at the glass of white wine in my right hand. "My name's Sarah, Sarah Williams. I'm thirty-four years old, and I'm from California. But you don't want to hear about me," I say, and the smile slowly leaves my face. "In fact, you really don't want to talk to me **at all**[5]. You see, I'm not a very interesting person." I laugh, but it is a sad and lonely sound. "This train journey is probably the most interesting thing that I've ever done."

I hold the glass of wine up to the light and move it slowly in a circle. "Although, I do have one story that I could tell you.

1 **to roll past** – *(hier) vorbeiziehen*
2 **emptiness and nothingness** – *Leere und Bedeutungslosigkeit*
3 **to avoid sb.**– *jdn. meiden*
4 **thought** – *Gedanke*
5 **at all** – *überhaupt*

It's probably the only interesting story that I have, and you're very lucky, because it's a story about something that happened to me **just**[1] yesterday."

For a moment, I wait, and listen to the sound of the train as it moves across the valley. It almost sounds like it's saying my name, I think. Sarah. Sarah. Sarah. Sarah.

I can't listen to that. So I start my story, and I don't care if my new **acquaintance**[2] is even **paying attention**[3] to me anymore.

"It was yesterday evening. I was sitting at **this very**[4] table, but I was alone. I had my book with me, but I wasn't reading it. Instead, I was enjoying the conversations of the other passengers. People are so different when they're travelling, don't you think? They talk about subjects that they usually never talk about. They laugh and smile more.

Anyway[5], it was nearly eight o'clock, and the sun had set over the distant Rocky Mountains. I was enjoying my second glass of wine, when I noticed a woman sitting at a table on the other side of the **aisle**[6].

As soon as I saw her, I couldn't look away. She was the most beautiful woman in the world. She had **curly**[7] black hair, green eyes, and skin as white and pure as snow. And she was elegant. Her little black dress and **high-heel shoes**[8] made her look like a movie star from the 50s.

I tried to move my eyes back to my book, but I was **enchanted**[9]. Then, while I was watching her, I saw her do the strangest thing. She had a glass of whisky in her right hand, but her left hand was empty, and by her side. Slowly, this hand began to move backwards; like a pure white snake, I thought.

1 **just** - *gerade (eben), erst*
2 **acquaintance** - *Bekanntschaft*
3 **to pay attention to sb.** - *jdm. (seine) Aufmerksamkeit schenken*
4 **this very** - *eben dies(-e, -er)*
5 **anyway (ugs.)** - *aber egal; jedenfalls*
6 **aisle** - *Gang*
7 **curly** - *lockig*
8 **high-heel shoes** - *hochhackige Schuhe, Stöckelschuhe*
9 **to be enchanted** - *entzückt sein, verzaubert sein*

Before I knew what she was doing, I saw her reach into the handbag of the woman behind her and take the woman's purse.

I **was** so **amazed**[1].

From the corner of my eye, I watched this beautiful woman open the purse, look through it, remove something, then close it again.

Then, with the same **skill**[2] as before, she returned the purse to the woman's handbag and smiled.

It was the most amazing smile that I have ever seen. So **confident**[3]. So **content**[4].

But I was still watching her when the smile **disappeared**[5], and I **realised**[6] that the woman was now looking directly at me.

Suddenly, I was afraid.

I tried to make it seem like I was reading my book; that I had seen nothing.

But she knew. I knew that she knew."

I stop talking and take a **sip**[7] of my wine. I enjoy the momentary silence and let myself **glance at**[8] the interested expression on my listener's face.

"Well, I didn't know what to do. If I got up and walked away, the woman would know for sure that I had seen everything. Was she dangerous? Was she a criminal? There was something about her that made me think of the attractive female **villains**[9] that you see in the old **spy movies**[10].

I was still thinking about what I should do, when suddenly I saw the mysterious woman **rise elegantly**[11] from her table and walk towards me.

1 **to be amazed** - *verblüfft sein, erstaunt sein*
2 **skill** - *(hier) Geschicklichkeit*
3 **confident** - *selbstbewusst*
4 **content** - *zufrieden*
5 **to disappear** - *verschwinden*
6 **to realise (that) (BE), to realize (that)** - *erkennen, (, dass)*
7 **sip** - *Schluck*
8 **to glance at sth.**- *auf etw. schauen*
9 **villain** - *Schurke, Verbrecher(in)*
10 **spy movie** - *Spionagefilm*
11 **to rise elegantly** - *elegant aufstehen*

For a moment, I thought that she would walk straight past me.

But she didn't. Instead, without a word, she **slipped into the seat**[1] opposite me, just where you're sitting now, and with a voice as **seductive**[2] as any I can imagine, she said '*Funny, isn't it, what you see from the corner of your eye sometimes*?'

And then she smiled, and it was such a smile that **I couldn't help but**[3] copy it, and before I knew it we were laughing, too.

She wouldn't tell me her name, but she spoke to me in the greatest of details about the long, **seemingly endless**[4] journey that she was on, the cities that she had visited, the men and women that she had met, the lovers that she had left.

Finally, when we were finishing our second drink together, she took something from her handbag and placed it on the table in front of me. 'I'm not a **thief**[5],' she said. 'At least, not the type of thief that you think I am. I never take their money or their bank cards. Only this. Only the one thing that they give away so easily every day. Only their names.'

It was a **driving license**[6], but it was not hers.

'**Variety**…' she said '… **is the spice of life**[7]. Do you know that **expression**[8]?'

I nodded my head, suddenly nervous again.

'I take their names, that's all. I **borrow**[9] them. Why do we have to live our lives with only one name? We don't wear only one dress. We don't visit only one city. We don't take only one lover. Do we?'

1 **to slip into a seat** - *in einen Sitz hineinrutschen*
2 **seductive** - *verführerisch*
3 **I couldn't help but …** - *Ich konnte nicht anders als …*
4 **seemingly endless** - *scheinbar endlos*
5 **thief** - *Dieb(in)*
6 **driving license** - *Führerschein*
7 **Variety is the spice of life.** - *Abwechslung gibt dem Leben erst die (nötige) Würze.*
8 **expression** - *Ausdruck, Wendung*
9 **to borrow sth.** - *etw. ausleihen*

And those **terrifying**[1], fantastic green eyes **burnt**[2] into me with an intensity I had never felt.

I had questions for her, of course, but she didn't let me ask them. Instead, we left the dining car together and went back to my **private compartment**[3]."

I stop talking again, and I notice for the first time that my acquaintance's glass of wine is nearly touching my own, that her fingers are only centimeters from my hand. She's pretty, I think, for the first time. Her long red hair like fire in the light of the afternoon sun.

"Well, I could tell you more about my time with that mysterious lady, but I don't think that I will. In the morning, when I woke, she was gone. I looked for her at breakfast. I walked to the viewing areas of the train. She was nowhere. It was like she never **existed**[4]."

I stop and smile at the woman across from me.

"But I didn't mind. It was an adventure. Like I said before, I'm not a very interesting person, so I'm happy that I got to meet such a strange **character**[5] on this short trip of mine."

I take another sip of my wine and **shrug**[6]. "There, that's my story."

Across the table, the woman **leans back**[7] and smiles. "I liked it. I liked it very much. Was it all true?"

I **frown**[8]. "Of course? Why?"

"Oh, just because I thought for a moment that maybe the woman in the story was you. You said that she had curly black hair and green eyes."

"She did."

1 **terrifying** - *furchterregend*
2 **to burn** - *brennen*
3 **private compartment** - *Privatabteil*
4 **to exist** - *existieren*
5 **character** - *Person, Wesen*
6 **to shrug** - *mit den Schultern zucken*
7 **to lean back** - *sich zurücklehnen*
8 **to frown** - *die Stirn runzeln*

The woman smiles. "But so do you." I turn to the window of the train and see my **reflection**[1]. "Oh no," I laugh. "No, she was beautiful. I'm nothing like her. I wish I was."

The woman moves her fingers and touches my hand. "Well, I think you're very beautiful, Sarah," she says, quietly.

For a moment, I say nothing, her hand still on mine. "You never told me your name," I say.

"Robyn," she replies. "And I wish I could talk to you some more, but I'm **getting off**[2] at Jasper, and the train will be stopping there in just a few minutes. **Unless**[3] Jasper is your stop, too."

I look at her again. She is really quite attractive. There's something sweet and **innocent**[4] about her kind blue eyes and **delicate lips**[5].

"Maybe. I don't know," I say.

Her fingers move away from mine and she stands. "There's a bar across from the station at Jasper, it's called the Black Dahlia. I always go there for a drink after a long journey. Always." I smile at her and watch her walk away, then I stand myself and move in the other direction, back towards my private compartment.

When I reach the door, I feel suddenly **guilty**[6], like I have done something wrong.

"I'm back," I say, as I open the door. "Sorry I took so long."

I move into the compartment and stand there for a moment.

Robyn. What a beautiful, wonderful name, I think. It's a name that makes me think of open skies and distant countries.

I turn and look at myself in the mirror. She's right, my hair is black and curly, my eyes are green. And I'm wearing a little black dress and elegant high heels. Was I wearing this yesterday? I don't know. I can't remember.

1 **reflection** – *Spiegelbild*
2 **to get off** – *aussteigen*
3 **unless** – *außer*
4 **innocent** – *unschuldig*
5 **delicate lips** – *zarte Lippen*
6 **guilty** – *schuldig*

For a moment, **my mind fills with confusion**[1]. I try to remember who I am. I try to remember my name.

My name. Sarah? Alice? Jane? Veronica? Sophia? Claire?

A **dozen**[2] faces appear in my memory, but I can't remember why. Emptiness fills me and that horrible feeling of nothingness makes me think that I'm going mad.

Slowly, the feeling **passes**[3], but I know that it will return again soon.

I open my purse and take something from it. I don't want it anymore. I thought that I did, but **I'm bored**[4] of it already.

Funny, I think, how quickly I become bored of them these days. Much quicker than I used to.

I can feel the train beginning to slow down. This is it. Jasper.

I think about the whisky that I'll order when I get to the Black Dahlia and I smile.

Robyn. Yes. What a beautiful name.

Happy now, I walk to the thin **cupboard**[5] in the corner of the compartment, open it slightly, no more than **the tiniest of cracks**[6], and I look at the thing in my hand. It's a driving license. And in the corner of the license there is a picture of a pretty young blonde with a **tanned**[7] face and blue eyes.

"Goodbye, Sarah," I say to the picture. "It was nice to meet you, but there's so much more out there for me to see and do." And I let the license fall into the darkness of the cupboard. "**After all**[8]," I whisper, "variety is the spice of life."

Then I close the cupboard, turn, and leave the small compartment without looking back.

And the compartment is silent and empty, and there is nothing strange about it at all.

1 **sb.'s mind fills with confusion** - *jd. ist (mit einem Mal) verwirrt*
2 **dozen** - *Dutzend*
3 **to pass** - *vorbeigehen*
4 **to be bored of sth.** - *von etw. gelangweilt sein*
5 **cupboard** - *Schrank*
6 **the tiniest of cracks** - *ein klitzekleiner Spalt*
7 **tanned** - *braun gebrannt*
8 **after all** - *schließlich*

Apart from[1], perhaps, the long blonde hairs which **are trapped**[2] at the bottom of the cupboard door, and the thin **trickle of blood**[3] that is slowly moving down the hair, and **dripping**[4] onto the clean white carpet below.

Eine der beliebtesten Eisenbahnstrecken Kanadas führt von **Toronto** im Südosten des Landes nach **Vancouver** im mittleren Westen. Auf einer viertägigen Zugfahrt können Reisende einen fantastischen Eindruck davon gewinnen, welch abwechslungsreiche und atemberaubende Landschaften dieses riesige Land zu bieten hat. Die Bahnstrecke der luxuriösen Langstreckenzüge führt an einigen der schönsten Gegenden Kanadas entlang. Man kann diese romantische Reise auch wunderbar bei einem Glas Wein und einem guten Buch genießen. Da wird die Zugreise auch schnell zu einer Zeitreise zurück in die Filmszenarien eines *Film Noir* der 1940er Jahre, wo man leicht auf eine der gefährlichen *Femmes Fatales* treffen konnte, die so typisch für diese Art Kriminalfilm sind.

1 **apart from** - *abgesehen von*
2 **to be trapped** - *(hier) eingeklemmt sein*
3 **trickle of blood** - *dünner Blutfaden*
4 **to drip** - *tropfen*

6. IN THE DARK

For a moment, the **cave**[1] is dark and empty, and only the **occasional**[2] **drips of water**[3] that fall from the **stalactites**[4] make any noise in the silence.

Then, from a small tunnel at the south end of the large space, a light **appears**[5], and there is the sound of movement.

Soon, a man appears. He is tall and slim, with a grey beard, long nose, and an unhappy expression on his serious face.

"Come on! Hurry up," he shouts. Then he stands up and looks around the cave with the light that is attached to his **helmet**[6].

After a moment, an attractive woman appears at the **mouth**[7] of the tunnel, her pretty face dirty, the long red hair under her helmet a **tangled mess**[8].

"Where are the others?" the man **snaps**[9].

"They're coming, Max," she says, as she stands and tries to smile.

Max Webber, **CEO**[10] of Webber Incorporated, shakes his head and turns back to the tunnel. "Hurry up, you **pathetic worms**[11]!"

"Max, you can't speak to them like that," the woman says.

A dark expression moves across Max's face, and he **takes hold of the woman's arm**[12]. "I can speak to them any way I like, Tracey. I'm their boss. And I'm your boss, too. Don't forget that."

1 **cave** - *Höhle*
2 **occasional** - *gelegentlich*
3 **drips of water (Pl.)** - *Wassertropfen*
4 **stalactite** - *Stalaktit, Tropfstein*
5 **to appear** - *erscheinen*
6 **helmet** - *Helm*
7 **mouth** - *(hier) Öffnung, Eingang*
8 **tangled mess** - *zerzaustes Durcheinander*
9 **to snap** - *blaffen, schimpfen*
10 **CEO (chief executive officer)** - *Generaldirektor(in); Geschäftsführer(in)*
11 **pathetic worm** - *armseliger Wurm, armseliger Wicht*
12 **to take hold of sb.'s arm** - *jdn. am Arm packen*

The woman tries to smile again. "I just meant, well, this **is supposed to be**[1] a team-building weekend."

Max lets go of her arm and laughs. "Team-building? Ha! With these **disloyal**[2] idiots?"

Tracey looks at her boss. "Disloyal?"

"Yeah, disloyal. I got an email from our **accountants**[3] this morning. Someone is **stealing from**[4] me. Hundreds of thousands of pounds. And it's one of these three idiots. I know it."

"I can't believe it," Tracey says.

"Believe it. When we get back to London, I'm going to find out which of them it is. Then…"

There are more sounds of movement in the tunnel, and Max stops talking. "Don't say a word about this," he says quietly. "You might be good at **keeping my bed warm**[5], Tracey, but not so good that I won't fire your pretty little **arse**[6]."

Then, from the tunnel, three more people slowly appear, each of them dirty, tired, and unhappy.

"God, look at you **lot**[7]," Max snaps. "My top management team. Fat Phil, Lazy Larry, and Stupid Sarah."

Phil, a middle-aged man with a round stomach, laughs. "You're right, Max. I do need a bit more exercise."

"*You're right, Max,*" Max **mimics**[8]. "Jesus, you really are a worm, Phil."

"So, have you been in these caves before, Max?" asks Larry, a short, younger man, with glasses on his face.

"Of course I have. I grew up in Wales. I know the Daren Cilau caves better than you know the back of your own hand."

1 **sth. is supposed to be sth.** - *etw. soll etw. sein*
2 **disloyal** - *treulos, illoyal*
3 **accountant** - *Buchhalter(in)*
4 **to steal from sb.** - *jdn. bestehlen*
5 **to keep sb.'s bed warm** - *jdm. das Bett wärmen*
6 **arse (vulg.)** - *Arsch*
7 **lot (ugs.)** - *Truppe, Haufen*
8 **to mimic sb.** - *jdn. nachahmen*

“Oh, good. We were just a bit worried. I mean, don’t we need a **guide**[1] to show us the way?” says Sarah, a middle-aged woman with nervous brown eyes.

“A guide?” Max shouts, and his voice **echoes**[2] around the cave. “Pathetic!” He looks at the three managers again and shakes his head.

“So,” says Tracey, with another weak smile. “Where next?”

“There,” says Max, who points to another tunnel at the east side of the cave. “And try **to keep up**[3] this time.”

And Max Webber moves to the mouth of the new tunnel and climbs inside.

Phil is about to follow him when Tracey **grabs**[4] his arm and pulls him back. “Wait!” she **whispers**[5], then listens to the sound of Max as he moves **further**[6] down the tunnel.

“What?” asks Sarah, her eyes even more nervous.

Tracey waits for a few more seconds, then looks at the three managers. “He knows.”

“Impossible!” says Larry.

“Shh...!”

“What do you mean?” asks Phil.

“What do you think? He knows about the money. He just told me.”

“But… but… how?” asks Sarah.

Tracey looks at her angrily. “I don’t know! Ask Larry. It was his idea.”

“No it wasn’t. It was yours. I just told you how it could be done… in theory.”

“Jesus, what have we done?” asks Phil.

“We’re going to prison. We’re all going to prison!” Sarah says in a loud voice.

1 **guide** - *Reiseführer, (hier) Höhlenführer*
2 **to echo** - *(wider)hallen*
3 **to keep up (with sb.)** - *(mit jdm.) Schritt halten, (mit jdm.) mithalten*
4 **to grab sth.** - *nach etw. greifen*
5 **to whisper** - *flüstern*
6 **further** - *weiter*

Tracey's hand **slaps across the other woman's face**[1]. "Shut up!"

"What are you doing?" They hear Max shout from the tunnel.

Tracey moves to the mouth of the tunnel. "It's Sarah. She felt a bit ill. But she's okay now. We're coming."

"Pathetic!" they hear Max **roar**[2].

Tracey moves back to the others, her eyes angry. "Now listen to me, you **stupid cowards**[3]. No one is going to prison. You just have to do what I say."

"Do what?" asks Phil, as **sweat**[4] starts to **pour down**[5] his pink face.

"Look where we are, Phil. Use your brain for once. These caves are dangerous. Anything could happen down here," Tracey whispers. "Anything."

Nobody says anything, but the silence of the cave is enough of an answer for Tracey. "I'll do it. I know none of you **have the backbone for it**[6]. All you have to do is say that it was an **accident**[7]. Do you understand?"

Phil and Larry slowly nod their heads, but Sarah is too scared to move.

"Sarah, we stole nearly a million pounds. If we don't do this, our lives are over. Do you understand?" Tracey repeats, her eyes carefully watching the other woman.

"I… I… yes," she finally says.

Tracey looks at the three managers again. Max is right. They really are pathetic worms.

Then she turns to the tunnel and begins to follow the man **she is about to**[8] kill.

1 **to slap sb. across the face** – *jdm. ins Gesicht schlagen, jdm. eine klatschen*
2 **to roar** – *brüllen*
3 **stupid coward (ugs.)** – *dummer Feigling*
4 **sweat** – *Schweiß*
5 **to pour down** – *hinunterfließen, hinunterrinnen*
6 **to have the backbone for sth.** – *das Rückgrat für etw. haben, sich etw. trauen*
7 **accident** – *Unfall*
8 **to be about to do sth.** – *gerade etw. tun wollen, im Begriff sein etw. zu tun*

As Tracey **wriggles through**[1] the rocks, with Max in front and the three managers behind her, she begins to think.

Yes, Max has to die. She has known this for some time now. For weeks she has thought about how to do it. A little poison in his evening whisky. A problem with the **brakes**[2] on his car. A **pillow**[3] on his face as he sleeps.

But now, all of her plans will have to change.

She can make it look like an accident, she is almost certain that she can. The caves are dangerous. The rocks are wet. Max could **slip**[4] and fall.

All she has to do is wait for the right place. Then she can move up behind him and…

Bye-bye Max.

No more keeping his bed warm at night.

She almost smiles, but then she hears the sound of the other three behind her.

Idiots. Max is right about that. Stupid, lazy… disloyal?

Can she **trust**[5] them to keep their mouths shut?

Tracey isn't sure. Maybe Phil and Larry… but Sarah?

Yes, it's a problem.

Maybe, she thinks, as she sees light at the end of the tunnel. Maybe it would be easier if all four of them had a little accident. Maybe Max falls. Then, when Phil and Larry and Sarah aren't looking…

All four of them? The idea is almost too terrible to **consider**[6].

Almost.

"Come on!" Max shouts, and his face appears at the mouth of the tunnel.

Tracey climbs out into the **darkness**[7].

1 **to wriggle through sth.** – *mit Mühe über etw. klettern, sich durch etw. hindurchwinden*
2 **brake** – *Bremse*
3 **pillow** – *(Kopf)kissen*
4 **to slip** – *ausrutschen*
5 **to trust sb.** – *jdm. (ver)trauen*
6 **to consider sth.** – *etw. in Erwägung ziehen, etw. in Betracht ziehen*
7 **darkness** – *Dunkelheit*

"Careful," Max snaps. "**Big drop down there**[1]." And the CEO points down to a large **chasm**[2] in the rocks.

Tracey steps forward to look. It's a large **pit**[3], at the bottom of which hundreds of **stalagmites**[4] point up into the air like **ancient**[5] **swords and daggers**[6].

When she sees it, a smile **spreads across**[7] her mouth.

"Yes, it's quite **impressive**[8]," says Max. Tracey stops smiling. "Yes. Yes, it is."

Behind her, the idiots slowly move out of the tunnel.

"Be careful here," says Tracey. "There's a big drop. We don't want any accidents." And she moves the light on her helmet so that the three managers can see the deadly stalagmites in the pit below.

"Ha!" Max laughs. "Maybe it's better if they all fall down there. Then I can find some employees who actually know how to do their jobs."

"So where now, Max?" she asks, and she moves closer to the CEO.

"We go along the side of the pit, here," he says, and points to a **thin ledge**[9].

"It looks a bit wet. Are you sure that it's safe?"

"Jesus, you're as bad as these worms," he says. "Look, it's perfectly fine." And the CEO steps onto the thin ledge at the side of the pit.

"I don't know if I **dare**[10] walk across that, Max. Could you help me?"

And Tracey puts out her hand.

1 **big drop down there** - *hier geht es steil nach unten (drop = Höhenunterschied, Gefälle)*
2 **chasm** - *Spalte*
3 **pit** - *Grube*
4 **stalagmite** - *Stalagmit, Tropfstein*
5 **ancient** - *alt*
6 **swords and daggers** - *Schwerter und Dolche*
7 **to spread across** - *sich breitmachen über, sich ausbreiten über*
8 **impressive** - *eindrucksvoll, beeindruckend*
9 **thin ledge** - *schmaler Felsvorsprung*
10 **to dare (to) do sth.** - *sich trauen etw. zu tun*

It's now or never, she knows.

Max looks at her angrily, but then he **reaches out his hand**[1], and Tracey notices how close he is to the edge.

Their fingers touch. She has to be careful. She doesn't want to fall in there, too.

"Come on! Hurry up!" Max snaps.

Then, as he tries to pull her forwards, Tracey suddenly pulls his hand back, and the taller man **stumbles**[2] towards her. Quickly, with the force of her shoulder, she **rams**[3] him to the side, his feet slip on the wet rocks of the cave, and for a moment Max Webber, CEO of Webber Incorporated, **hangs in mid-air**[4] above the deadly pit, an expression of complete surprise on his face.

His hands reach out for something to hold, but Tracey only smiles.

Then the CEO falls back, and a second later there is a **horrendous**[5] **crunch**[6] at the bottom of the pit.

"Ha-ha!" Tracey laughs, amazed at how easy it was. "Bye-bye, Max!" she shouts into the darkness. "Bye-bye and thanks for all the money! I hope your new bed is nice and warm!"

"Is he...?" she hears Phil ask. "Are you sure he's…?"

Tracey laughs again. "Dead? Of course he is."

"But can you see him?" Larry asks.

Tracey moves a little closer to the edge of the pit and looks down at the horrible sight below.

"Oh yes, we don't have to worry about him anymore."

"Excellent," says a voice in her ear, and she quickly turns around. Sarah is standing right in front of her, but there is something very different about her. Her usual nervous expression is not there. Instead, she **looks extremely confident**[7] and relaxed. "Sarah?"

Sarah smiles. "Thanks for all your help, Tracey. You were a real

1 **to reach out one's hand** - *seine Hand ausstrecken*
2 **to stumble** - *stolpern*
3 **to ram** - *rammen, stoßen*
4 **to hang in mid-air** - *halb in der Luft hängen*
5 **horrendous** - *schrecklich, entsetzlich*
6 **crunch** - *Knirschen*
7 **to look extremely confident** - *überaus selbstsicher aussehen*

team-player, but we just don't need you anymore." Then Tracey feels the older woman push her, and the next thing she knows she is falling backwards into the pit. She thinks she feels the stalagmites as they **explode**[1] through her back. She thinks that she hears the sound of **laughter**[2] from the ledge above. But the one thing she is sure of, as the life slowly leaves her body, is that she is once more lying next to Max Webber; and there seems to be a **satisfied smile**[3] on the old man's **cruel**[4] face.

Die **Daren Cilau Höhlen** liegen im Süden von **Wales**. Dieses Paradies für Höhlenforscher erstreckt sich auf eine Gesamtlänge von über 26 Kilometern und gehört damit zu den größten Höhlen des Landes. 1957 wurden die Höhlen von Vic Howells entdeckt. Zu ihren imposantesten Teilen gehören die sogenannte *Time Machine* (Zeitmaschine) - der größte Höhlendurchgang Großbritanniens - und die *White Company* (die weiße Gesellschaft) - eine Tropfsteinformation aus blütenweißen Stalaktiten.

Das Höhlensystem ist so weitläufig, dass man mehr als 20 Stunden darin verbringen und verschiedene Routen erkunden kann. Aus diesem Grund hat man für den Höhlentourismus mittlerweile feste Lager darin errichtet.

Die Höhlen dürfen nur mit professionellem Tourguide betreten werden. Allerdings gab es auch schon übermütige Höhlenforscher, die sich nicht an die Regeln gehalten haben und im steinernen Meer verloren gegangen sind.

1 **to explode** - *zerbersten, (hier) sich bohren*
2 **laughter** - *Gelächter*
3 **satisfied smile** - *zufriedenes Lächeln*
4 **cruel** - *grausam*

7. THE BOX

The limousine stops in front of the **entrance**[1] to JFK airport, and Jane feels her **stomach**[2] **tighten with anxiety**[3].

Kane tells his driver to wait, then he pushes a button and the dark **glass screen**[4] rises and **separates**[5] the front of the limousine from the back.

"So, here we are," Kane says, and he smiles at Jane.

He's a handsome man, about forty years old, with dark hair and **tanned skin**[6].

But when he smiles Jane feels her anxiety increase. It's not the smile of a good man. It's the smile of a snake, a crocodile, a dangerous animal.

"You look good," he says, and his cold eyes move from her long legs and grey dress, to her short blonde hair and blue eyes.

Jane tries to smile. "But Kane..." "No," he says, in a quiet voice, and his smile **disappears**[7]. "Listen to me. Listen very carefully. You're a beautiful girl, Jane. Very beautiful. You're a good dancer, too. The guys at the club all love you." He **leans forward**[8] and puts a hand on her leg. "But you stole from me, darling. You stole twenty thousand **bucks**[9] from me."

"I'm sorry, Kane. I really am. I **was desperate**[10]. I needed it..."

Kane moves his hand from her leg. For a moment he's silent, then he smiles again. "I know, darling. I know you're sorry. And

1 **entrance** - *Eingang*
2 **stomach** - *Magen*
3 **to tighten with anxiety** - *sich vor Sorge zusammenziehen*
4 **glass screen** - *Glasscheibe*
5 **to separate** - *abtrennen*
6 **tanned skin** - *sonnengebräunte Haut*
7 **to disappear** - *verschwinden*
8 **to lean forward** - *sich vorlehnen*
9 **bucks (Pl., ugs.)** - *Kröten (Geld)*
10 **to be desperate** - *verzweifelt sein*

that's why you're here. That's why I didn't do anything to you. I didn't hurt you. I didn't call the **cops**[1]."

And Jane wants to laugh, because she knows that Kane would never tell the cops anything.

"You see," he continues. "I know you want to do something to show me that you're really sorry; something to make me forget about the twenty thousand bucks. And this is it, darling, this one small thing. You do this, and I forget everything. You can keep your job at the club. You can even keep some of the money." Jane says nothing. She hates dancing at Kane's horrible club, but she makes good money there. And she needs money. She needs it for her expensive dresses, for her dinners at **luxurious**[2] New York restaurants, for the parties that she goes to almost every night.

"But what do I have to do, Kane?" "Do? Nothing, darling. I just want you to fly to London for the weekend and stay in a nice four-star hotel."

Jane waits, because she knows that there is more.

"And because you're going to London," Kane says, and his horrible pink **tongue**[3] moves across his **lips**[4]. "You can take something to an old friend of mine."

Jane watches him open the **briefcase**[5] on the seat next to him and take out a small black box. For a moment, Kane looks at it, a strange and horrible expression in his dark eyes. It's an expression that she has never seen in those eyes before. She is not sure if it is **fear**[6] or **disgust**[7], but she knows it means there is **something extremely terrible**[8] inside that box.

"Easy. You take this box to London, and I forget everything."

Jane looks at the box for a moment, then she opens her mouth to ask something.

1 **cops (Pl., ugs.)** - *Bullen, Cops*
2 **luxurious** - *luxuriös*
3 **tongue** - *Zunge*
4 **lip** - *Lippe*
5 **briefcase** - *Aktentasche, Aktenkoffer*
6 **fear** - *Angst, Furcht*
7 **disgust** - *Ekel*
8 **something extremely terrible** - *etwas ganz Fürchterliches*

"No," Kane says, before she can speak. "**You don't get to**[1] ask me any questions about this box. And you don't get to open it. Do you understand?"

Jane **nods**[2].

"All you need to know, is that it's very important that this box gets to my old friend in London. There's something in there that I know he's going to want to see." And Kane smiles, but there is still that strange expression in his **cruel**[3] eyes. "Now, show me your **carry-on bag**[4]." Jane shows him the small black **suitcase**[5] that she has brought with her.

"Open it."

Inside, there are two dresses, an extra pair of shoes, a book, some **underwear**[6], and a camera.

"Good. That's good. Now put the box inside; carefully. Then forget about it. Do you understand? Forget the box is there. Just **go through security**[7] with a smile on your pretty face, and there won't be a problem."

"But Kane, what if they stop me? What if they want to see inside the box?"

Kane's handsome face becomes dark and dangerous again. "No one can see inside that box. You're a beautiful girl, Jane. You can **distract**[8] the security guards if you need to. But Jane, darling, understand this. If that box doesn't arrive in London by ten o'clock tomorrow morning, you're going to be very sorry. And maybe you think you can run, and maybe you think you can hide, but you can't."

He looks at his watch. "Now get out of the car," he says, and he opens the door for her without another word.

1 **You don't get to ...** - *Du wirst nicht/Sie werden nicht ...!*
2 **to nod** - *nicken*
3 **cruel** - *grausam*
4 **carry-on bag** - *Reisetasche; Handgepäck*
5 **suitcase** - *Koffer*
6 **underwear** - *Unterwäsche*
7 **to go through security** - *die Sicherheitskontrolle passieren*
8 **to distract sb.** - *jdn. ablenken*

Outside, the sun is hot and high, and for a moment Jane stands and looks at the **impressive**[1] glass entrance to JFK airport.

"Don't **disappoint**[2] me, Jane," Kane says. Then the door closes and the limousine moves away.

Slowly, her carry-on bag in her hand, she walks to the entrance of the airport and moves in the direction of the check-in desk.

She knows that Kane is going to kill her if she doesn't take the black box to London, but she also knows that there is something terrible inside the horrible little thing. Something that even Kane does not want to look at.

She needs to think, and when she sees a bar she knows that a drink will help to calm her anxiety and **clear her mind**[3].

She finds an empty table and orders a large glass of white wine.

Can she leave the box somewhere? Pass through security without it? Find a new job in England? Forget about New York and her expensive dresses and **amazing**[4] parties?

Maybe. But she remembers Kane's **promise**[5] that he will find her, and she knows that he will.

No. She has to think. She has to be clever.

And then she sees him; a short man with blonde hair, an expensive suit, and silver sunglasses. He is sitting at the table next to hers. He has a newspaper in his hands, but his eyes aren't looking at the newspaper; they are looking **directly**[6] at her legs.

Normally, she would tell the **creep**[7] to stop looking, but when she sees the small black carry-on next to his chair, **an idea begins to form**[8] in her **mind**[9].

1 **impressive** - *beeindruckend*
2 **to disappoint sb.** - *jdn. enttäuschen*
3 **to clear sb.'s mind** - *jds. Kopf frei machen*
4 **amazing (ugs.)** - *toll*
5 **promise** - *Versprechen*
6 **directly** - *genau, direkt*
7 **creep (ugs.)** - *Widerling*
8 **an idea begins to form** - *allmählich eine Idee haben*
9 **mind** - *Geist, Kopf; Gedanken*

"Excuse me?" she says.

The man quickly moves his eyes from her legs. "Yes?"

"Are you flying to London? To Heathrow?"

For a second the man is silent. "Well, actually, yes, I am."

"Do you know what **gate**[1] the flight is **departing**[2] from?" The man smiles and looks up at the large electronic screens. "Sure, gate 42."

"Oh, that's great." And she moves her leg a little and watches his eyes follow it. "Are you going on holiday?"

"Yeah," he says, putting his newspaper down on the table. "Just for a few days."

"Really? What a **coincidence**[3], me too," she says. "And are you travelling alone?"

The man's smile **fades**[4] a little. "No. I'm travelling with a… friend."

"Oh, I see. Your girlfriend?"

His face becomes a little pink. "Oh no, just a friend."

Jane smiles again. "Good."

It's a simple idea, but she is sure that it can work. If she can distract the man, she can **exchange**[5] their bags. Then she can wait near to the security area and watch him go through. If there's a problem, she can leave quietly, get on a train to Canada, and try to escape from Kane.

But if there's no problem, she can find him at gate 42, **apologise**[6], and exchange the bags again.

The man is so distracted by her legs that she is sure it will be easy to make the exchange.

She looks at her glass of wine. Yes, that can work.

1 **gate** - *Flugsteig, Gate*
2 **to depart** - *abfliegen*
3 **coincidence** - *Zufall*
4 **to fade** - *(hier) (ver)schwinden*
5 **to exchange sth.** - *etw. austauschen*
6 **to apologise (BE), apologize** - *sich entschuldigen*

"And do you..." she begins to say, then she moves her arm, hits her glass of wine, and **spills it onto**[1] the table.

"Oh no! I'm so **clumsy**[2]," she says.

"Let me get you a **cloth**[3]," the man **offers**[4].

"Thank you. You're so **kind**[5]." As soon as the man turns his back and starts to walk to the bar, Jane moves from her seat, her bag in her hand, and exchanges it with the other bag next to the man's table.

They look **identical**[6], she thinks, as she quickly returns to her seat and places the man's bag next to her.

This can really work.

"Here you are," he says, as he returns from the bar with the cloth.

"You really are so kind. Would you like to sit down for a moment?"

And Jane is not surprised when the man **accepts her invitation**[7].

For a while they sit and talk, and Jane does everything that she can to **keep** the man's **attention on her**[8], and not on the carry-on bag that he is about to take through security.

"Maybe I can call you in London?" she asks, after a few minutes. "We could meet for a drink."

"I would love to, but I think I'll be too busy," his hand is on her arm now. "But maybe when we return to New York?" "That would be great." The man smiles. "Excellent."

"Well, I have a few things that I need to buy, but I'll see you at the gate," Jane says, with one final smile.

1 **to spill sth. onto sth.** - *etw. auf etw. (ver)schütten*
2 **clumsy** - *tollpatschig, ungeschickt*
3 **cloth** - *Lappen*
4 **to offer** - *anbieten*
5 **kind** - *freundlich*
6 **identical** - *identisch, genau gleich*
7 **to accept an invitation** - *eine Einladung annehmen*
8 **to keep sb.'s attention on sb.** - *jds. Aufmerksamkeit weiterhin auf jdn. gerichtet halten*

And when she walks from the table Jane can feel the man's eyes on her legs again, and she laughs, because she thinks that this is almost too easy.

"James!" a woman's voice says.

"What? Oh, Adele." And the man quickly moves his eyes from the legs of the beautiful woman in the grey dress who is walking away from the table and looks at the person who is now standing next to him.

"James, you were looking at that woman!"

"What? No, don't be **silly**[1]. Do you want a drink, babe?"

Adele, a short woman with long brown hair and a serious face, sits down at the table. "Do we have time?"

"Sure," James says. "Our flight to Paris is at four." He orders two more drinks, but sees that his girlfriend looks extremely angry.

"You know you're the only woman for me, babe," he says, but she doesn't smile.

Then he remembers the **gift**[2] in his carry-on bag; the **silver necklace**[3] that he knows she wants.

"Babe, look in my bag. There's a little surprise in it for you," he says with a large smile.

Adele opens the bag, but stops when she sees the dresses and shoes. "James, what are these?"

But James doesn't look. "The black box. Do you see it? It's for you. Just a small thing."

And Adele takes the black box out of her hands.

"Open it," James says.

"What is it?"

"Just open it," he repeats.

1 **silly** - *dumm*
2 **gift (AE)** - *Geschenk*
3 **silver necklace** - *silberne (Hals)kette*

And the **scream**[1] that fills the bar at the entrance to JFK is so loud, and so terrible, that Jane hears it.

But no one looks at her as she starts to run from the airport.

No one looks at her; because everyone is looking at the screaming woman, and the terrible thing in the small black box that she is holding in her hands.

Der Flughafen John F. Kennedy, der meistens nur JFK genannt wird, ist der belebteste Passagierflughafen Nordamerikas. Er liegt in **New York** und hieß früher Idlewild. Der Name wurde allerdings 1963 zu Ehren des ermordeten Präsidenten Kennedy geändert.

Der Flughafen hat sechs Terminals und 128 Gates. 2016 wurden dort beinahe 59 Millionen Passagiere abgefertigt.

Obwohl der Flughafen eines der weltweit größten Security-Teams hat, sind Verbrechen durchaus nicht unüblich. Kleinere Verstöße wie Taschendiebstahl oder Gepäckdiebstahl sind an der Tagesordnung. Doch das ist nicht alles, denn auch schwerere Verbrechen wie Drogen- oder Waffenschmuggel halten die Sicherheitsbeamten auf Trab. Außerdem gibt es auch immer wieder Versuche, exotische Tiere oder sogar menschliche Körperteile illegal durch die Sicherheitskontrollen zu schleusen.

1 **scream** – *Schrei(en), Geschrei*

8. COFFIN BAY

The man on the high **stool**[1] at the bar puts down his pen, picks up his half-full glass of cool beer, and takes another long drink.

He is a short young man with **thinning brown hair**[2], serious grey eyes, and a nervous, unhappy expression on his face.

In front of him, on the bar, is a dark leather notebook, the pages of which are filled with **scruffy writing**[3].

Occasionally, the man puts down his beer and writes something in the notebook. Then, with a quiet **curse**[4], he takes the pen and **crosses out**[5] the words.

After some time, he throws the pen onto the notebook and looks around the bar.

There are very few people in the Anchor this evening.

A young couple are sitting at a corner table in their beach clothes, their **tanned**[6] faces close together and their expressions **carefree**[7].

At another table, three middle-aged men **are playing dice**[8] and shouting at the cricket game on the television.

Apart from that, the only other people are the few individuals who, like the man at the bar, seem happy to sit alone and enjoy their drinks.

The young man turns back to the bar and **taps** his finger **against**[9] his now empty glass.

1 **stool** - *Hocker*
2 **thinning brown hair** - *schütteres braunes Haar*
3 **scruffy writing** - *schlampige Schrift*
4 **curse** - *Fluch*
5 **to cross out sth.** - *etw. ausstreichen*
6 **tanned** - *sonnengebräunt*
7 **carefree** - *sorglos*
8 **to play dice** - *ein Würfelspiel spielen*
9 **to tap against sth.**- *gegen etw. tippen*

"Another one?" the large woman at the end of the bar asks.

The man, whose name is Eddie, **nods his head**[1].

The large woman smiles, moves off her stool, and walks to the back of the bar. "You don't say much, **do ya**[2]?" the woman says. "You've been in here every night for a week, and I don't remember you saying more than ten words. What's wrong with ya?"

Eddie **shakes his head**[3]. "Nothing to say."

The woman's smile **disappears**[4]. "Oh yeah? Well, some people round here would say that's not very friendly."

Eddie **shrugs**[5]. "Well, I'm not from round here."

The woman laughs. "Oh, I know that. English, are ya?"

Eddie nods, **aware**[6] that several of the people in the bar are now listening to the conversation. "Yes. From London."

The woman shrugs. "Oh well. We **don't mind**[7] **the pommes**[8] too much."

Several people in the bar laugh, then turn back to the TV or their own thoughts.

"On holiday?" the woman asks, as she passes Eddie his new beer.

"Not really. I'm a writer. I'm here **to do… research**[9]."

The woman smiles again. "Research? Sitting in a bar drinking beer. **Sounds like**[10] a holiday to me."

Eddie says nothing, but passes her five dollars.

The woman laughs, then moves back to her stool at the far end of the bar.

1 **to nod one's head** – *(mit dem Kopf) nicken*
2 **…, do ya? (ugs., Kurzform von 'do you')** – *… oder?*
3 **to shake one's head** – *den Kopf schütteln*
4 **to disappear** – *verschwinden*
5 **to shrug** – *mit den Schultern zucken*
6 **to be aware that** – *sich bewusst sein, dass*
7 **to not mind sb.** – *nichts gegen jdn. haben*
8 **the pommes (vulg.)** – *die Briten*
9 **to do research** – *Nachforschungen anstellen*
10 **to sound like sth.** – *wie etw. klingen*

Annoyed[1], Eddie takes a long drink of his beer and turns back to his notebook, his pen in his hand.

"An English writer in Coffin Bay?" a voice next to him says.

A tall, middle-aged man, with a tanned and **weathered**[2] face is now standing next to his stool. "Well, that's not something we see every day." The man smiles and **holds out his hand**[3]. "I'm Parker. It's nice to meet you."

For a moment, Eddie doesn't move. **The last thing he needs**[4] is more **distractions**[5] from his work. After a few seconds, he takes the man's hand and quickly shakes it. "Eddie," he **mumbles**[6], and hopes that this will be enough to make the man go away.

"Eddie? Eddie what? Have you written anything I might know?"

"Probably not," Eddie says, and he picks up his pen.

The man pulls out a stool and sits down on it. "Oh yeah? And what type of thing do you write?"

Eddie **sighs heavily**[7] and puts down the pen. "Crime fiction."

The man **whistles**[8] and a large smile **spreads across**[9] his face. "Really? Well, I like a good crime novel. Here, Lizzy, get me and Eddie another beer," the man shouts to the bar lady.

"I'm okay, thank you. I have a beer."

"Okay. Two whiskeys then," Parker smiles, and Eddie **notices**[10] the three gold teeth at the front of his mouth.

"I really don't have time. I'm trying to write."

"Oh yeah? Is this your new novel then?" Parker says, **pointing to**[11] the notebook. "It looks like you're having a bit of trouble."

1 **to be annoyed** - *genervt sein*
2 **weathered** - *wettergegerbt*
3 **to hold out one's hand** - *die Hand ausstrecken*
4 **the last thing sb. needs** - *das Letzte, was jd. braucht*
5 **distraction** - *Ablenkung*
6 **to mumble** - *murmeln*
7 **to sigh heavily** - *schwer seufzen*
8 **to whistle** - *pfeifen*
9 **to spread across** - *sich breitmachen über*
10 **to notice sth.** - *etw. bemerken*
11 **to point to sth.** - *auf etw. (hin)deuten*

The bar lady, Lizzy, places two whiskeys down in front of them. "Leave him alone, Parker. He said he's trying to work," she says, before she walks away.

"Maybe I can help. What's the problem? You need some ideas about how to kill someone?" And the older man **flashes his gold teeth at**[1] Eddie again.

Eddie shakes his head. "That's always the easy part."

Parker grins. "Yeah. I guess it is. So maybe your problem is what to do with the body."

Eddie is a little surprised, but he tries not to show it. "**Actually**[2], yes. That's exactly the problem."

Parker laughs. "Well, it all depends on where you kill someone. Kill someone in a desert and you **bury**[3] them. Kill someone in a city, that's difficult. You have to **chop the body up**[4] or **dissolve it in acid**[5]. Where's your novel **set**[6]?"

Eddie normally doesn't like to talk about his work, but the beers have relaxed him and he thinks that it might be interesting to hear the local man's opinion. "Well, it's set in a small town in Australia."

"What? Really? Like Coffin Bay?" Parker laughs again. "Well then you don't have a problem at all!"

"What do you mean?"

"Well, look out that window there, Eddie. What do you see?"

Eddie looks out of the window at the other side of the bar. Outside, the evening sun is slowly disappearing into the **vast**[7] Indian Ocean.

He shakes his head. "You can't just throw a body into the ocean. **Even if**[8] you **put weights on it**[9], there's the possibility the

1 **to flash one's teeth at sb.** - *jdm. gegenüber ein Zahnfleischlächeln aufsetzen*
2 **actually** - *wirklich, tatsächlich*
3 **to bury sb.** - *jdn. begraben*
4 **to chop the body up** - *die Leiche zerstückeln*
5 **to dissolve sth. in acid** - *etw. in Säure auflösen*
6 **to be set (novel)** - *stattfinden, (hier) spielen*
7 **vast** - *riesig*
8 **even if** - *selbst wenn*
9 **to put weights on sth.** - *Gewichte an etw. hängen*

tide[1] might push it back to the **coast**[2]. I want this to be a perfect murder. I need to know that the body will never be found."

Parker laughs again and **slams** his whiskey **down**[3] onto the bar. "Oh but Eddie, this is Coffin Bay. Don't you know what Coffin Bay **is famous for**[4]?"

Eddie shakes his head.

"Well then look at this."

Then the older man stands up and **lifts up**[5] his grey shirt to **reveal**[6] his stomach. There, on his tanned skin, is a long white **scar**[7] in the **shape**[8] of a large semi-circle.

"Jesus. Is that...?"

"Shark bite, Eddie. Ten years old."

For the first time, Eddie is now interested in the conversation. "And are there sharks in this area?"

Parker moves closer to the writer and quickly looks around the bar. "There are, but **keep your voice down**[9]. We don't like to talk about them. Sharks aren't good for tourism."

Eddie nods his head and speaks a little more quietly. "And these sharks. Could they…? I mean… Could they eat an **entire**[10] body?"

Parker's face is now very close, and Eddie can smell the beer and whiskey on the other man's **breath**[11]. "Oh yes, Eddie. If you know the right **spot**[12]. If you **chum the water**[13]. If you make sure there are four or five of those beauties… they'll eat anyone you throw to them."

1 **tide** - *Gezeiten, (hier) Flut*
2 **coast** - *Küste, Ufer*
3 **to slam sth. down** - *(hier) etw. hinknallen*
4 **to be famous for sth.** - *für etw. berühmt sein*
5 **to lift up sth.** - *etw. hochheben*
6 **to reveal sth.** - *etw. (her)zeigen, etw. enthüllen*
7 **scar** - *Narbe*
8 **shape** - *Form, Gestalt*
9 **to keep one's voice down** - *leise sein*
10 **entire** - *ganz, gesamt*
11 **breath** - *Atem*
12 **spot** - *(hier) Ort, Platz*
13 **to chum the water** - *das Wasser mit Ködern versehen*

A small smile starts to appear on Eddie's face. "Well that could work. That could be perfect. A murder in a small town. The body is never found because the murderer **feeds it to**[1] the sharks. It's original. It's exciting[2]."

Parker laughs again and takes another drink. "I told you I could help."

The smile disappears from Eddie's face. "But can it really work? I mean *really*? I want this to be perfect."

Parker nods his head. "Sure it can. Hell, I could take you out on my boat right now. I could show you a perfect spot."

"Really?"

"Sure. And because it's you, I'll only **charge a** very small **fee**[3]."

"A fee? How much?"

Parker sits back down and thinks for a moment. "Well, there's the money for the petrol, the **chum**[4] that we need **to attract**[5] the sharks. Then there's a bit of money for my time. I mean, it might take us an hour to get to the good spot. Even then, you might not actually see a shark."

"How much? How much? The money's not important. I just want to see how it can be done. I just want the story to be perfect."

Parker smiles when he hears the **enthusiasm**[6] in the other man's voice. "Well, two hundred dollars would be what we call **mates rates**[7]."

"Two hundred? That's fine. I have that with me." And Eddie takes out his **wallet**[8] and pulls two hundred dollars from it.

1 **to feed sth. to sth.** - *etw. an etw. verfüttern*
2 **exciting** - *aufregend, spannend*
3 **to charge a fee** - *eine Gebühr berechnen*
4 **chum** - *(hier) Köder*
5 **to attract** - *anlocken*
6 **enthusiasm** - *Begeisterung*
7 **mates rates (Pl., ugs.)** - *Freundschaftspreis*
8 **wallet** - *Geldbörse, Brieftasche*

Parker looks at the wallet and sees the many other hundred dollar **bills**[1] that are in there. "Great," he says, with an even bigger smile.

"And can we go now? Right now?"

Parker looks out of the window at the **setting sun**[2]. "This is the perfect time to go, Eddie. The sharks are always **near the surface**[3] of the water at this time of day."

Eddie closes his notebook and takes the glass of whiskey from the bar. "Then let's go."

Parker **raises**[4] his own glass and the two men drink.

"Go wait for me outside, Eddie. I just have to pay my bill."

Eddie picks up his notebook and moves towards the door. "This is great. Thank you, Parker. This is exactly the type of research I need. This story has to be perfect. It has to be… real."

And with a large smile on his face the Englishman leaves the bar.

The Australian watches him go and walks over to Lizzy.

"**Nice one**[5], Lizzy," he says quietly. "The **bloody fool**[6] has more money than sense."

Lizzy whispers. "I told you. He must have about five thousand dollars in that wallet. What are you going to do?"

"I'll see how much money I can get from him. I'll tell him there are some other good places I can show him tomorrow. See if I can take him out a few more times, too. I **bet**[7] I can get another three hundred dollars from him."

Lizzy laughs and gives her husband a kiss on the lips. "Nice one, Parker. Don't forget to buy me something good with the money."

"Of course not, darling," the fisherman says.

1 **bill** - *Geldschein*
2 **setting sun** - *untergehende Sonne*
3 **near the surface** - *in der Nähe der Oberfläche*
4 **to raise sth.** - *etw. heben*
5 **Nice one! (ugs.)** - *Gut gemacht!, Nicht schlecht!*
6 **bloody fool (ugs.)** - *dummer Idiot*
7 **to bet** - *wetten*

Then, as Parker leaves the bar, a large smile on his face, Lizzy turns and looks at the television. The cricket match has just finished, and the news is starting.

"Well, we don't want to hear this **rubbish**[1], do we **lads**[2]?"

And the bar lady picks up the **remote**[3] and **turns the volume down**[4].

The three men at the table return to their game of dice, the couple in the corner continue to **stare**[5] into each other's eyes, and Lizzy walks behind the bar and **pours herself a** large **whiskey**[6].

And no one looks at the television again.

So no one sees the picture of a short man with thinning brown hair and serious grey eyes. And no one hears the warning that the **news presenter**[7] is giving; that there have been **several sightings**[8] of an extremely dangerous criminal in the South of Australia.

The criminal, the news story explains, is an English **serial killer**[9], who police believe has killed more than five people. **Completely psychotic**[10], the criminal kills in extremely strange ways and is very good at **disposing of**[11] the bodies of his **victims**[12].

But no one in the bar hears this.

And outside, under the red light of the setting sun, the motor of a small boat starts.

But no one hears this either.

1 **rubbish** - *Müll*
2 **lads (Pl., ugs.)** - *Jungs*
3 **remote** - *Fernbedienung*
4 **to turn the volume down** - *etw. leiser stellen*
5 **to stare** - *starren*
6 **to pour oneself a whiskey** - *sich einen Whiskey einschenken*
7 **news presenter** - *Nachrichtensprecher(in)*
8 **several sightings (Pl.)** - *einige Beobachtungen*
9 **serial killer** - *Serienmörder(in)*
10 **completely psychotic** - *völlig psychotisch*
11 **to dispose of sth.** - *etw. beseitigen, etw. loswerden*
12 **victim** - *Opfer*

→ Die Austernstadt **Coffin Bay**, was auf Deutsch übersetzt so viel heißt wie *Die Bucht der Särge*, liegt an der Südküste Australiens auf der dreieckigen Eyre-Halbinsel. Außerhalb der Saison leben hier gerade einmal 500 Einwohner, aber im Sommer versechsfacht sich die Bevölkerung, und dann tummeln sich Schwimmer, Surfer und Wasserskifahrer an den wunderschönen Stränden.

Ein wahres Paradies, so scheint es zumindest auf den ersten Blick, hätte **Coffin Bay** nicht auch eine Schattenseite: Leider tummeln sich nicht nur Touristen an den Stränden, sondern auch Haie in den Gewässern. Immer wieder gab es in der Vergangenheit Berichte über Haiattacken, bei denen Menschen nicht nur schwer verletzt, sondern auch getötet wurden.

9. THE FOURTH CLUE

They say that before you die your whole life **flashes before your eyes**[1], but it's not my life that I think about as the **bullet**[2] races towards my heart; it's this case. This **damn**[3] case.

Did I get it right in the end? Or did I make a mistake?

The **clues**[4] were there, three of them.

Or perhaps I should say four, because wasn't there **one final piece to this puzzle**[5]?

Yes, the final piece... was her.

She comes into my office like she owns it, and there's only one word to describe her: perfect. Her elegant dress, her long blonde hair, those big serious blue eyes. All perfect.

But perfect can **be trouble**[6], so I keep things professional. I let her do the talking. I let her start this whole thing.

"Detective Collis, my husband **has disappeared**[7]. I need you to find him."

"It's Mr Collis," I say. "I'm not with the police anymore."

"But you are a detective? A private detective."

"Sure," I say, and I offer her a chair. "So what do the cops say about your husband?" I ask.

"Nothing. They say they can't help."

"Is there another woman?"

1 **to flash before one's eyes** - *vor den (eigenen) Augen vorbeiziehen*
2 **bullet** - *Kugel*
3 **damn (vulg.)** - *verflucht*
4 **clue** - *Hinweis*
5 **one final piece to the puzzle** - *letztes fehlendes Puzzlestück*
6 **to be trouble** - *für Unruhe sorgen, Schwierigkeiten bedeuten*
7 **to disappear** - *verschwinden*

"Perhaps. You know what men are like." And the way she looks at me across my desk **makes my blood hot**[1]. "But he has something of mine; an old family **heirloom**[2]. I want it back."

"So get a divorce. Get the court to give it back to you."

"I can't wait that long. It has **sentimental value**[3]."

"What is it? Jewels? Gold?"

"No, it's the other half of this." And she takes a strange **mahogany statue**[4] from her bag. It's the size of my hand and in the **shape**[5] of a snake. "There are two of these. He has the other, and I want it back."

"Do you have any idea where he is?"

"No, but I have these," she says, and she passes me a **file**[6]. Inside there are three items; a **serviette**[7] with a date and time **scribbled on**[8] it, a list of flights to countries around the world, and an **overexposed**[9] Polaroid picture of something almost impossible to see. "I printed off the list from his work computer. The other two things I found in the bottom of his suitcase." "He didn't take his suitcase?" "No, he didn't take anything." And I hear **concern**[10] in her voice for the first time. "He travels a lot. He has clients all around the world. But he never takes pictures. He says views are better with your own eyes."

"He's right," I say, and I let my eyes exam the **gentle curve**[11] of her neck. "So, you want me to find him. If he's in trouble, you want me to get him back. If he's with another woman, you want the statue. Is that about right?"

She almost smiles. "I see I've found the right man for the job."

1 **to make sb.'s blood hot** - *jds. Blut in Wallung bringen*
2 **heirloom** - *Erbstück*
3 **to have sentimental value** - *einen ideellen Wert haben*
4 **mahogany statue** - *Mahagonistatue*
5 **shape** - *Gestalt, Form*
6 **file** - *Aktenordner, (Akten)mappe*
7 **serviette** - *Serviette, Stofftaschentuch*
8 **to scribble on sth.** - *auf etw. kritzeln*
9 **overexposed** - *überbelichtet*
10 **concern** - *Besorgnis, Sorge*
11 **gentle curve** - *zarte Wölbung*

"Yeah, and how did you find me?"

"Old friends. They said you were good."

Yeah, I *was* good; but that was a long time ago. What about now?

That night, I go back to my cold Seattle apartment, and I try to be the detective she needs me to be.

Three clues.

The **flight list**[1] is almost useless. The husband **has flown**[2] to more than twenty countries in the last year; Tokyo, London, Paris, Sydney.

And the serviette tells me little, too. The date is the fifth of May, the time seven-thirty, and there are only three other words; *wait for me*.

There is, however, **the slightest scent of**[3] expensive perfume, so I hold it to my nose and **breathe deeply**[4].

Then I pick up the photo and look at it under the light from my lamp. It's overexposed, the image almost impossible to see. Perhaps there's a river next to a strange building, but perhaps not.

I decide that I need a drink, so **I pour myself a** large **whisky**[5]. And for a while I drink and smoke, the three clues on the table in front of me, thoughts of Mrs Perfect and her perfect smile in my mind. Finally, I pick up the statue of the snake. She told me to take it with me, **to keep it safe**[6], to keep it with me **at all times**[7], because it has a deep sentimental value to her.

I begin to **move my fingers over it**[8], my mind wandering. I'm about to put it down and pour myself another whisky when a smile slowly moves across my face, and I think for the first

1 **flight list** - *Flugliste*
2 **to fly** - *fliegen*
3 **the slightest scent of sth.** - *(ein) zarter Hauch von etw.*
4 **to breathe deeply** - *tief einatmen*
5 **to pour oneself a whiskey** - *sich (selbst) einen Whiskey einschenken*
6 **to keep sth. safe** - *etw. sorgfältig aufbewahren*
7 **at all times** - *stets*
8 **to move one's fingers over sth.** - *seine Finger über etw. bewegen*

time that maybe I understand **what** this case **is all about**[1]. That maybe I *can be* the detective that she needs me to be.

But first, I need to understand the three clues.

So I drink a little more, and I smoke a little more, and I pick up the picture to **examine**[2] it with my tired eyes, and suddenly I see it. Suddenly I know where to go.

"Nice work, Detective Collis," I say to myself.

I open a suitcase, throw in a few clothes, the three clues, and the statue of the snake. She told me to take it with me. She told me she wanted me to be sure that I could **recognise**[3] the other statue without any problem.

For a moment, I look at the snake and smile.

And then I sleep.

Because by this time tomorrow, I need to be in London.

The bullet hits me in the **chest**[4] and the **pain**[5] is impossible to describe. I don't **realise**[6] for a second that it pushes me from my feet and my head hits the glass floor. **Beneath**[7] me, I can see black taxis and red buses, but nobody looks up. The gun **was silenced**[8], the noise impossible to hear from anywhere but the empty **viewpoints**[9].

For a moment, I move between **consciousness**[10] and **unconsciousness**[11], and I remember how I got here.

I remember the airport in Seattle; the first time I know for sure that **I'm being followed**[12]. And I remember the security

1 **what sth. is all about** - *wovon etw. handelt, worum es bei etw. geht*
2 **to examine sth.** - *etw. überprüfen; genau ansehen*
3 **recognise (BE), recognize** - *(wieder)erkennen*
4 **chest** - *Brustkorb*
5 **pain** - *Schmerz*
6 **to realise (BE), realize (that)** - *erkennen (, dass)*
7 **beneath** - *unter*
8 **to silence** - *dämpfen (Schall)*
9 **viewpoint** - *Aussichtspunkt*
10 **consciousness** - *Bewusstsein*
11 **unconsciousness** - *Bewusstlosigkeit*
12 **to be followed** - *verfolgt werden*

check, and how they look at the **contents**[1] of my bag before they let me through.

I don't remember the flight, except that I drink to make it go faster, and that at one point I feel someone watching me again; but I don't look round.

And in London I try **to keep out of sight**[2]. I organise one or two things. I drink English beer in a quiet pub. I look up at the tower.

The tower where I now lie with a bullet a few centimetres from my heart.

"The statue," the voice repeats, and the **figure**[3] with the gun steps from the **shadows**[4] of the viewpoint of London's Tower Bridge, a hat and coat hiding their face.

I want to laugh because the figure looks like a character from an old black and white film, but I don't because my chest hurts too much, and I need to know if I'm right about everything.

The figure moves, the gun still **pointing at**[5] me, and they pick up my bag and remove the statue.

"You... were... following me," I say.

The figure **nods**[6].

"You can speak. I know it's you. I can smell your perfume from here."

There's a moment of silence, and I watch the gun as I lie there on the floor.

She takes the hat from her head and her blonde hair falls down to her neck. She looks different, no makeup, no pretty dress; but she couldn't **resist**[7] the perfume.

1 **contents (Pl.)** – *Inhalt*
2 **to keep out of sight** – *sich verstecken; sich versteckt halten, sich nicht sehen lassen*
3 **figure** – *Person*
4 **shadow** – *Schatten*
5 **to point at sb.** – *auf jdn. zeigen*
6 **to nod** – *nicken*
7 **to resist sth.** – *etw. widerstehen*

"Of course I was following you. I didn't want to take the statue through **customs**[1] myself, but I had to make sure it was safe at all times."

"You're clever."

"A Polaroid picture and a list of countries. You didn't make it easy for me."

She smiles. "But you're here. And so is my statue. I knew you would bring it for me. Perhaps I could have brought it myself, but why **risk it**[2]? It's much easier to make some idiot like you carry it for me. I didn't want to shoot you, but you didn't give it to me when I asked."

And she takes the statue and she presses a **hidden switch**[3] and a small door opens in the wood.

"So what is it? What do you and your husband **smuggle**[4] from country to country? Drugs, diamonds?"

She laughs. "Husband? There is no husband. There is no other statue. There's only me. This is my business, and I don't smuggle anything as common as drugs or diamonds. I **deal in**[5] information. Government secrets, **corporate espionage**[6]. And I have enough information on this **memory stick**[7] to..."

She stops, and she looks into the hole in the statue.

"Where is it?" she **whispers**[8], and the gun points at me again. "Where's the memory stick?"

For a moment I don't say anything, but I **take a deep breath**[9] and slowly start to stand up. She might shoot me again, but unless she **aims for my head**[10], I'll be okay. The **bulletproof vest**[11]

1 **customs (Pl.)** - *Zoll*
2 **to risk sth.** - *etw. riskieren*
3 **hidden switch** - *versteckter Schalter*
4 **to smuggle** - *schmuggeln*
5 **to deal in sth.** - *mit etw. handeln*
6 **corporate espionage** - *Wirtschaftsspionage*
7 **memory stick** - *Speicherstick*
8 **to whisper** - *flüstern*
9 **to take a deep breath** - *tief einatmen*
10 **to aim for the head** - *auf den Kopf zielen*
11 **bulletproof vest** - *schusssichere Weste*

that the London police gave me is enough to stop the bullets of her small revolver.

"Thank you for the confession, that's all we need." "We? What do you mean?"

But Mrs Perfect doesn't seem to understand.

"Three clues? What do you think this is? An old detective novel? I knew something was wrong the moment you came into my office. You were just *too* perfect. And too perfect is always trouble. Rich, beautiful women don't hire **down-on-their-luck detectives**[1] like me. And it didn't take me long to realise your statue was a box. The moment you told me to take the statue with me, I thought something was wrong. You said it was a family heirloom, but you let me, a complete stranger, take it half the way round the world for you? It just **didn't make sense**[2].

The Seattle police department has your memory stick now, and they told the airport security to let me pass. You thought I was following your clues like an idiot. You thought I didn't know you were following me." I laugh again. "The hat and coat confused me though, until I smelt the perfume. I thought maybe I was wrong, and that there was a husband, but thanks to your **confession**[3] we now know it's only you."

She starts to lift the gun again, but then the London police appear, **their own guns raised**[4].

"It's over, **sweetheart**[5]," I say, and I watch her as they take her away.

Then I turn and look at the grey city and the dark but **impressive**[6] River Thames.

She's right about one thing, I think, as I **let the wind take**[7] the Polaroid picture; views are better with your own eyes.

1 **down-on-their-luck detectives (Pl.)** – *abgehalfterte Privatdetektive*
2 **not to make sense/to make no sense** – *keinen Sinn ergeben*
3 **confession** – *Geständnis*
4 **their own guns raised** – *mit erhobenen Waffen*
5 **sweetheart (ugs.)** – *Schätzchen*
6 **impressive** – *beeindruckend*
7 **to let the wind take sth.** – *den Wind etw. davontragen lassen*

→ Die **Tower Bridge** ist eines der berühmtesten Bauwerke **Londons**. Die 240 m lange und 65 m hohe Brücke wurde zwischen 1886 und 1894 erbaut und offiziell am 30. Juni 1894 vom Prinzen und der Prinzessin von Wales eröffnet. Zwei Fußgängerstege verbinden die beiden Türme miteinander und liefern den Besuchern einen fantastischen Blick über London und die Themse. Auf dieser Fußgängerverbindung befindet sich auch ein Museum über die Geschichte der Brücke. Außerdem sind einige Teile des Bodens aus Glas, so dass man direkt auf die Themse und den Verkehr hinabblicken kann.

Die Tower Bridge wird jedoch nicht nur als eines der bekanntesten Wahrzeichen Großbritanniens angesehen, sondern gilt auf der ganzen Welt als ein Symbol für Stärke und Gerechtigkeit.

10. THE MAGPIE

There's a worried expression on the face of Chief Inspector Sean O'Brien, and **every now and then**[1] he quickly moves his hand through his short grey hair; an old **habit**[2] that he has when he is thinking very hard about a difficult problem.

Normally, the chief inspector shows little emotion, and he never lets his officers see that he's worried about a case.

At the moment **though**[3], he's alone, with no one near to him to see these little **signs of nervousness**[4].

Well, almost alone, he thinks.

He's standing at a large window in a dark room. Behind the window, in a separate room, a middle-aged woman with long **auburn**[5] hair and gentle brown eyes is sitting at a small table, her hands **cuffed together**[6] and a **recording device**[7] in front of her.

But she can't see him, he thinks.

At least, she shouldn't be able to. But from time to time he's sure that he feels her eyes move in his direction.

This is impossible though, he knows. It's **two-way glass**[8]. For him it's a window, for her, nothing more than a large mirror.

Still, every now and then he's sure that those gentle brown eyes **linger on him**[9] for a while, and the smallest of smiles appears at the corner of her mouth.

1 **every now and then** - *hin und wieder, ab und zu*
2 **habit** - *Gewohnheit*
3 **though** - *jedoch*
4 **sign of nervousness** - *Zeichen von Nervosität*
5 **auburn** - *rotbraun*
6 **to be cuffed together** - *in Handschellen gelegt sein*
7 **recording device** - *Aufnahmegerät*
8 **two-way glass** - *Einwegspiegel*
9 **to linger on sb. (eyes)** - *(hier) auf jdm. ruhen*

He moves back from the window and looks at the **file**[1] on the desk in front of him. He's about to open it when there's a knock on the door.

"Enter," he calls, his professional, **calm expression**[2] on his long thin face again.

The person who enters the room is a shorter, younger man with tired eyes and a **tanned**[3] face. "Chief Inspector."

"Detective Pace?"

"Yes, sir. I'm sorry that the journey took me so long."

The inspector looks at his watch. "I think seven hours from New York to Dublin is pretty good, actually."

The American smiles. "I **would have been faster**[4], but there were crowds outside the station."

"Yes, well, there are a lot of **angry**[5] people out there."

"**I bet**[6]."

For a moment, neither man says anything. Then the inspector **points to**[7] the file on the table. "Thank you for sharing this information with us, Detective. **However**[8], I'm really not sure that it's the same woman."

Pace moves to the large window and looks into the next room, his eyes slowly **examining**[9] the woman who is sitting there.

For more than a minute he watches her, then, finally he turns back to the inspector and **shrugs**[10]. "I don't know what to say. As you can see from her file, we've never had a good picture of her. **Hell**[11], we've never had more than a few **blurred**[12] images."

1 **file** - *Aktenordner*
2 **calm expression** - *ruhiger Ausdruck*
3 **tanned** - *sonnengebräunt*
4 **to be faster** - *schneller sein*
5 **angry** - *wütend, zornig*
6 **I bet. (ugs.)** - *Bestimmt!, Garantiert!*
7 **to point to sth.** - *auf etw. zeigen*
8 **however** - *jedoch, aber*
9 **to examine sb.** - *jdn. prüfen*
10 **to shrug** - *mit den Schultern zucken*
11 **hell, ... (ugs.)** - *Mist, .., verdammt ..*
12 **blurred** - *unscharf, verschwommen*

"**And yet**[1] you came all this way?" says the inspector, who moves to stand next to him at the window.

"Well, you know that expression *a picture paints a thousand words*?"

"Of course."

"I never liked it. To me, it's actions that are important, not images, not words. As soon as I heard about the **theft**[2], I knew that it was her." The detective says. "I mean, a **robbery**[3] like this, in the middle of the day, alone? There's just no one else that could do it."

The inspector turns and looks at the other man. "You almost sound like you **admire**[4] her."

"Admire her? I've been looking for this woman for eight years. Three times she's **committed crimes**[5] in New York, **right under my nose**[6]. There are more than a few people in my department who think that's pretty funny, but I can tell you that my boss isn't one of them." The detective smiles and moves away from the window. "But yeah, inspector, I **guess**[7] I do **kind of**[8] admire her."

The chief inspector doesn't smile. "I can understand that, Detective. But if we don't solve this problem in the next twenty minutes, I have a feeling that no one will be laughing."

"Twenty minutes?"

"She's been here for nearly twenty-four hours. We can't keep her longer than that." The inspector says. "**After all**[9], we **don't have a scrap of evidence**[10] that she stole the **damn thing**[11]."

1 **and yet** - *aber dennoch, und doch*
2 **theft** - *Diebstahl*
3 **robbery** - *Raub(überfall)*
4 **to admire sb.** - *jdn. bewundern*
5 **to commit a crime** - *ein Verbrechen begehen*
6 **right under sb.'s nose** - *genau vor jds. Nase*
7 **to guess** - *vermuten*
8 **kind of** - *irgendwie*
9 **after all** - *schließlich; denn*
10 **to have not a scrap of evidence** - *nicht den geringsten Beweis haben*
11 **damn thing (vulg.)** - *verdammtes Ding*

"By *the damn thing*, you mean the **Nemain pin**[1]? How expensive is it?"

"Collectors say it's worth three million. But those crowds out there will tell you it's a **priceless**[2] part of Irish history. Personally, it just looks like a small piece of metal to me."

"And where could she sell something like that?"

"A few months ago, we had a report that someone was offering to sell the Nemain pin on the **dark web**[3]. We thought it was a joke, but we increased the security at the National Museum."

"And now it's gone."

"Yeah, and the whole of Ireland wants to know how."

Detective Pace **shakes his head**[4]. "That's what I don't understand. You said on the phone that the **press**[5] knew about the crime **straightaway**[6]. That they were waiting outside the museum when your men brought her out."

"That's right. It's just another thing about this **mess**[7] that I don't understand."

Pace looks through the window at the suspect and shakes his head. "Then I think we need to go and speak to the **Magpie**[8]."

And the two men turn and walk to the door.

"Hello again," says the chief inspector, as he steps into the **interview room**[9].

The two men move to the table. The Inspector looks at the clock on the wall, then presses a button on the recording device. "It's 15.25 and I'm restarting the interview. This is Detective

1 **Nemain pin** - *Anstecknadel bzw. Brosche mit der keltischen Sagengestalt und Göttin Nemain*
2 **priceless** - *unbezahlbar, von unschätzbarem Wert*
3 **dark web** - *Darknet*
4 **to shake one's head** - *den Kopf schütteln*
5 **press** - *Presse*
6 **straightaway** - *sofort, sogleich*
7 **mess** - *Durcheinander*
8 **magpie** - *Elster*
9 **interview room** - *(hier) Verhörraum*

Pace from the **NYPD**[1]. He's going to be **assisting with**[2] this **investigation**[3]."

The woman at the table looks at the clock on the wall, then turns to the inspector, and Pace sees **tears**[4] appear in her eyes. "Please, inspector. You have to listen to me," she says, her voice weak. "You have to believe me. This is all a terrible mistake. I'm **innocent**[5]. I'm not a **thief**[6]."

The two men sit down at the table. "Well, you've had a lot of time to think about what happened at the museum yesterday afternoon. Maybe now you can give us the information that we need."

"What information?" the woman asks, and the tears start to fall down her face. "I told you. I didn't see anything. There wasn't anyone else in the room with me." "Well that's the problem. We agree that there was no one apart from you there, which **means**[7] that you're our only suspect in this crime."

The woman begins to **sob**[8], and her cuffed hands move to her eyes. "But I didn't do anything."

"At exactly 14.35, yesterday, you were standing next to the **display case**[9] of the Nemain pin in the National Museum. At 14.36 you **raised**[10] your **umbrella**[11] and opened it. At that same moment, the alarm on the case **went off**[12] and security ran to your location. When they arrived, the display case was empty and the Nemain pin was gone."

"I know, I know! You've told me this a hundred times, but all I can tell you is that I didn't take it. I don't understand why

1 **NYPD (New York Police Department)** - *New Yorker Polizeirevier*
2 **to assist sb. with sth.** - *jdm. bei etw. helfen*
3 **investigation** - *(hier) Ermittlung*
4 **tear** - *Träne*
5 **innocent** - *unschuldig*
6 **thief** - *Dieb(in)*
7 **to mean** - *bedeuten*
8 **to sob** - *schluchzen*
9 **display case** - *Vitrine, Schaukasten*
10 **to raise sth.** - *etw. hochheben, etw. anheben*
11 **umbrella** - *Regenschirm*
12 **to go off (alarm)** - *losgehen*

you don't believe me. The **security guards**[1] **searched me**[2], the police searched me. I don't have the pin."

"Why did you open your umbrella?"

"I told you. It's an old umbrella. I was moving it from one hand to the other, and it **just opened**[3]."

"It just opened? It covered the view of you from the security cameras perfectly, but you say it just opened."

"You say your name's Laura Kelly," Detective Pace says. "Have you ever been to the US, Laura?"

The woman looks at Pace, and for the first time the American starts to think that he might have made a mistake. She **seems genuinely confused and afraid**[4]. "No. Never. I don't travel very much. Spain and France **now and again**[5]. Germany once. Why? Are you looking for an American woman?" Laura says, with an **unmistakeable**[6] Irish accent. "Is it someone that looks like me? Please, you must believe me. It's not me. I'm just an office worker from Killiney."

Pace says nothing for a moment. "There's an international thief called the Magpie. A woman, about your age. No one knows her real name, but they call her the Magpie because she **steals**[7] jewellery and other pretty things. We think that in total, over more than fifteen years, she's stolen more than **ninety million dollars' worth of property**[8]."

The woman looks at him for a moment. "And you think I'm her? You're crazy. I have a family, friends, a job."

The inspector nods his head. "She's telling the truth about that. **We've looked into it**[9]."

1 **security guard** – *Wachmann, Sicherheitsbeamter, -beamtin*
2 **to search sb.** – *jdn. durchsuchen*
3 **to just open** – *einfach aufgehen*
4 **to seem genuinely confused and afraid** – *wirklich verwirrt und eingeschüchtert erscheinen*
5 **now and again** – *dann und wann, von Zeit zu Zeit*
6 **unmistakeable** – *unverwechselbar, eindeutig*
7 **to steal** – *stehlen*
8 **ninety million dollars' worth of property** – *Eigentum im Wert von 90 Millionen Dollar*
9 **to look into sth.** – *etw. prüfen, etw. untersuchen*

"So you see, you've got the wrong person!" she says, and her eyes move to the clock on the wall again. "You can't keep me here. I want a **lawyer**[1]."

"We offered you a lawyer when we brought you here. You **refused**[2]."

"Yeah, yesterday, when I thought this was all a big mistake. How long have I been here for now? Nearly twenty-four hours. You can't keep me here."

The inspector takes his phone from his pocket and puts it on the table. "You **have the right to**[3] make a phone call, **Ms**[4] Kelly."

"But first, can you just tell me one more time what happened?" asks Pace.

The woman looks at him. "There's nothing to say. I was near the display case. I wanted to look at the pin, so I stepped forwards. At the same time, I moved my umbrella and it opened."

"And did you touch the case?"

For the first time, Pace sees a small smile appear at the corner of the woman's mouth, and he sees her look at the clock again, her eyes watching the **minute hand**[5] as it slowly moves. "You know. I don't remember."

"And then what?" asks the inspector.

"I heard the alarm. I moved away from the case and I waited. Then the security guards were there. They took me to a room and searched me. But they didn't find anything because I didn't have the pin. Then the police came."

"Did you see the pin in the case before the alarm?"

The woman **wipes the tears away**[6] and smiles at Pace again. "Oh yes. It's a fascinating piece of history."

1 **lawyer** – *(Rechts)anwalt, (Rechts)anwältin*
2 **to refuse** – *ablehnen, sich weigern*
3 **to have the right to do sth.** – *das Recht haben etw. zu tun*
4 **Ms** – *Frau (Bezeichnung, die für verheiratete und für unverheiratete Frauen gilt)*
5 **minute hand** – *Minutenzeiger (an der Uhr)*
6 **to wipe the tears away** – *(sich) die Tränen wegwischen*

Pace doesn't like that smile. All of a sudden there's something **devious**[1] and **cunning**[2] about it.

The inspector pushes his phone towards her, then reaches out and takes the cuffs from her hands. "Make a phone call, Ms Kelly. Call your lawyer or call someone to come and **pick you up**[3]."

"You're going to let me go?" she smiles.

Pace is about to speak, but the inspector puts his hand on his arm. "Yes, we are. We don't have any evidence to keep you here. But know this, Ms Kelly. We know what you **look like**[4]. We know where you live. Until I find that pin, we won't stop."

The woman takes the phone and **dials a number**[5]. After a second, she smiles and presses a button. Then, without a word, she ends the call.

"Thank you," she says, and she pushes the phone back to the inspector. "But there's someone waiting to collect me."

The two policemen look at each other, **puzzled**[6].

"And I wouldn't worry about the pin, gentlemen," she says, and Pace sees her eyes move to the clock again, and suddenly she seems very different. She doesn't seem confused and afraid anymore. She seems calm and **confident**[7]. "I think, when you look very closely at the case, you might find it."

"What do you mean?" asks the inspector.

The woman **stands up and stretches**[8]. "Well, what if someone put a very small but powerful **magnet**[9] on the side of the case? It would pull the pin to one side, where no one could see it."

1 **devious** - *hinterhältig, verschlagen*
2 **cunning** - *gerissen, schlau*
3 **to pick sb. up** - *jdn. abholen*
4 **to look like** - *aussehen wie*
5 **to dial a number** - *eine Nummer wählen*
6 **puzzled** - *verdutzt, verwirrt*
7 **confident** - *selbstbewusst*
8 **to stand up and stretch** - *aufstehen und sich strecken*
9 **magnet** - *Magnet*

Pace looks at the inspector. "Your men checked the case?"

"Of course. But it was empty and locked."

"They didn't look inside?"

The inspector shakes his head. "I don't know. It was chaos. Our priority was to make sure the pin didn't leave the museum. There were so many journalists trying to get inside."

"Yes," the woman smiles. "That was strange."

She walks to the door of the interview room. "Well, it's half-past three, gentlemen. That's twenty-four hours. Am I **free to go**[1]?"

The chief inspector moves his hand through his short grey hair. "**Let her go**[2], Pace. I need to call the museum," he says, as he picks up his phone.

Pace stands and walks to the door, his thoughts confused. "If the pin is still there, then you **failed**[3]."

"I think," the woman says. "You mean the Magpie failed. **Unless**[4], of course, she never wanted to steal the pin. Maybe she just wanted people to think it had been stolen. Maybe she was the one who called the press. Maybe, in the last twenty-four hours, **she's had people sell**[5] the pin three or four times on the dark web, to **naive criminals**[6] and **greedy collectors**[7] who will never get what they paid for."

Pace says nothing for a moment, but he opens the door and looks at the woman one last time. "I know what you look like now," he says, quietly. "I'll catch you. You know I will."

The woman smiles and steps out into the corridor. "You mean, you'll catch the Magpie? Oh, I don't know about that, Detective." And suddenly the woman's accent changes, and she sounds very American. "After all, Magpies are very clever birds."

1 **to be free to go** - *gehen dürfen*
2 **let sb. go** - *jdn. gehen lassen*
3 **to fail** - *versagen*
4 **unless** - *außer*
5 **to have people sell sth.** - *(einen) Verkäufer für etw. haben*
6 **naive criminals** - *naive Verbrecher*
7 **greedy collectors (Pl.)** - *(hab)gierige Sammler*

→ Das irische Nationalmuseum liegt in **Dublin**, der Hauptstadt der Republik Irland. Es ist bekannt für seine reichhaltige Sammlung irischer Kunst, Kulturgüter und naturkundlicher Exponate. Zu seinen archäologischen Ausstellungsstücken gehören prähistorische Exponate, frühe Goldartefakte aus der Zeit der Wikinger sowie religiöse Objekte, die über den Glauben und die Traditionen der frühen gälischen Kultur berichten.

Viele der Artefakte, die sich in diesem Museum wiederfinden, sind zweifellos von unschätzbarem Wert - aber sie sind es vor allem für die irische Bevölkerung, die sehr stolz auf ihr kulturelles Erbe ist.

11. ALL I WANT FOR CHRISTMAS

The room, on one of the top floors of the Meriton Suites hotel, seems empty for a moment, with only the sound of the Christmas songs on the record player to fill the silence.

Then, from the door of the bathroom, a man appears. He is tall and good-looking, with dark hair, **tanned skin**[1], and intelligent green eyes. On his **handsome**[2] face, there's a smile, and as he walks across the room he **whistles**[3] a **familiar**[4] Christmas song.

"That's right, baby," he says to the empty room. "All I want for Christmas… is you."

He stops at the elegant bar at one side of the room, **pours himself a** large **glass of**[5] vodka, drops two ice cubes into the alcohol, then walks to the mirror, the drink in his hand.

For a moment, he **inspects**[6] his clothes. His white shirt is perfectly **ironed**[7], the black trousers tight but not too tight, his new leather shoes **immaculate**[8].

"But if I'm lucky," he says to his **reflection**[9], "I won't be wearing any of this for too long."

He laughs at his joke and walks across the room, still singing the song. It's one of his favorites, he decides. In fact, when he hears her knock on the door, he might start the song again, so

1 **tanned skin** - *sonnengebräunte Haut*
2 **handsome** - *gutaussehend*
3 **to whistle** - *pfeifen*
4 **familiar** - *bekannt, vertraut*
5 **to pour oneself a glass of sth.** - *sich ein Glas … einschenken*
6 **to inspect sth.** - *etw. untersuchen, etw. überprüfen*
7 **to iron** - *bügeln*
8 **immaculate** - *makellos*
9 **reflection** - *Spiegelbild*

that he can sing a few of the **lyrics**[1] to her. Yes, she might like that. It might be a good way to **break the ice**[2].

He walks to the large window and looks out at the fantastic view. To the west, he can see the magnificent Bondi beach **stretch out**[3] into the night. To the East, the city of Sydney **twinkles**[4] with the Christmas lights that **decorate**[5] the streets and buildings. Somewhere in the distance, he thinks he can even see the part of the city where his small apartment is, but his building **is hidden by**[6] taller **skyscrapers**[7] and more elegant **tower blocks**[8].

Yeah, what a view, he thinks.

Then, for a moment, he almost starts to worry about how **ridiculously expensive**[9] the hotel room was.

But then he remembers his big Christmas bonus and he thinks about how well his company is doing at the moment.

You **deserve**[10] this, he says to himself, and he takes a big drink of vodka and smiles.

Anyway, you can't put a price on happiness, and **he's pretty sure**[11] that he's going to be very happy tonight.

He turns back to the room and looks at the large bed and the white gift box on top of it.

Oh yes, he thinks again, he's going to be very happy **indeed**[12].

It's then, however, that his phone rings, and his smile quickly disappears. He moves back to the bar, puts down his drink, and looks at the name on the screen of the phone.

1 **lyrics (Pl.)** - *(Lied)text*
2 **to break the ice** - *das Eis brechen; miteinander warm werden*
3 **to stretch out** - *sich erstrecken*
4 **to twinkle** - *funkeln*
5 **to decorate** - *schmücken*
6 **to be hidden by sth.** - *von etw. verdeckt werden; von etw. versteckt werden*
7 **skyscraper** - *Wolkenkratzer*
8 **tower block** - *Hochhaus*
9 **ridiculously expensive** - *aberwitzig teuer*
10 **to deserve sth.** - *etw. verdienen*
11 **to be pretty sure** - *sich ziemlich sicher sein*
12 **indeed** - *tatsächlich, wirklich*

For a moment, he feels a **stab of anxiety**[1], but he quickly pushes it away. "Come on, Martin," he says to himself. "You know what to say."

He reaches across to the record player, **lifts the needle**[2], then answers the phone.

"Hey, darling," he says, the tone of his voice heavy and unhappy. "Yeah, I know… look, I'm so sorry, but I won't be able to **get back**[3] tonight… no, I'm still in Perth… I know, darling, I'm sorry… no, the meeting was a disaster… No, of course I'll be back tomorrow… I promise… Yes, of course I want to spend Christmas Eve with you. You know that all I want for Christmas is you… Bonus? No, darling, not this year. I told you how bad things are at the moment… Yeah, I think I'll be doing quite a lot of **overtime**[4] in the next few months. Probably a bit of travelling too… yes, darling… okay… okay… I promise… Yes, I love you too, darling. See you tomorrow."

He ends the call, puts the needle back down on the record, and starts to whistle again, a large, **satisfied smile**[5] on his handsome face.

Poor Penny, he thinks. He loves her, in his own way. She's a great little wife, really. She's loyal, **trusting**[6], **obedient**[7]; everything a man wants in a woman.

Well, almost everything. He thinks about the long-legged, dark-haired Susan; the woman who he's waiting for. Yes, Susan has something that Penny doesn't; a **sensual**[8], dangerous **quality**[9]. As soon as he met her, he knew there was something a little crazy about her. Yes, there was a wild, crazy expression in her eyes. And sure, no one wants a crazy wife… but a crazy one-

1 **stab of anxiety** – *Anflug von Unsicherheit, Anflug von Panik*
2 **to lift the needle** – *die Plattenspielernadel anheben*
3 **to get back** – *zurückkehren; heimkommen*
4 **overtime** – *Überstunden*
5 **satisfied smile** – *zufriedenes Lächeln*
6 **trusting** – *treuherzig, vertrauensselig*
7 **obedient** – *gehorsam*
8 **sensual** – *sinnlich; erotisch*
9 **quality** – *Eigenschaft*

night-stand? Well, that would make it a very **merry**[1] Christmas indeed.

Martin laughs again, walks over to the bed, and looks at the white gift box. He reaches down and turns over the **gift tag**[2]. *To Susan from Santa. For being a very good girl.*

He's about to open the box and look at the sexy **lingerie**[3] inside, when he hears a quiet knock at the door.

Suddenly, he feels another stab of anxiety. He looks at his watch. Seven-fifteen? Is she really this early? A woman like her?

No. The champagne. It must be the champagne, he realises with a **relieved**[4] smile.

He moves the needle back to the start of the song, **just in case**[5] it is her, picks up ten dollars to give the **bell boy**[6] a **tip**[7], then walks to the door and opens it.

"Hi, thanks..." he starts to say.

But then he sees *her* face.

The eyes are different; bigger, wilder, red with tears, and **filled with an anger**[8] that he's never seen before. But it is *her* face.

"Bastard!" she **screams**[9].

Then she's moving forward, and there's something long and metal in her hand, but before he can stop her it **stabs into**[10] the top of his chest, just below his shoulder, and his **pain**[11] explodes in a terrible scream.

The next few seconds are like a nightmare. He falls backwards into the room. She follows him, her hand still on the knife, but she kicks the door closed, which stops his scream from escaping into the hallway.

1 **merry** - *fröhlich*
2 **gift tag (AE)** - *Geschenkanhänger, Geschenkschildchen*
3 **lingerie** - *Dessous, Damenunterwäsche*
4 **relieved** - *erleichtert*
5 **just in case** - *(nur) für den Fall (, dass)*
6 **bell boy** - *Hotelpage*
7 **tip** - *Trinkgeld*
8 **to be filled with anger** - *zornerfüllt sein*
9 **to scream** - *schreien*
10 **to stab into sth.** - *in etw. stechen*
11 **pain** - *Schmerz*

Then she's screaming too, and she pushes the knife so far into his **flesh**[1] that he thinks he feels it come out of his back.

Then he **trips**[2] and lands on the bed, and suddenly she's on top of him, that wild, crazy look in her eyes. She puts one knee on his stomach and tries to pull the knife out, but she can't. **Instead**[3], she reaches her other hand out to his face, her fingers **curled into claws**[4], and she **digs**[5] them into his eyes.

"Penny! No!" he shouts, the pain **impossible to bear**[6].

"Bastard! Bastard! Bastard! You **lying bastard**[7]!"

Even through the pain he understands, and his quick mind starts to work. "Penny, no! You don't understand!" He tries to push her off him, but his left arm is useless because of the knife, and his right one not strong enough to stop her **manic**[8] attack on his face.

"Penny, listen! Please! Please, darling, listen!" he shouts. And when she stops **for the briefest of moments**[9] his right hand strikes out and hits the side of her face, and her eyes seem to lose their wildness.

"Penny! Listen to me."

She looks at him, **blinks**[10], then the wildness returns. "You lying, bastard!"

But before she can reach for his eyes again, Martin moves his body, and with a scream his wife falls from the bed and hits her head against the corner of the bar.

Then Martin's moving quickly across the bed, unable to push himself up until he reaches the **edge**[11], and with another scream he falls forwards and lands on his knees. He looks at the

1 **flesh** - *Fleisch*
2 **to trip** - *stolpern*
3 **instead** - *stattdessen*
4 **to curl into claws** - *sich zu Krallen zusammenrollen*
5 **to dig** - *(hier) bohren; (ein)graben*
6 **to be impossible to bear** - *unerträglich sein, nicht auszuhalten sein*
7 **lying bastard! (vulg.)** - *dreckiger Lügner!*
8 **manic** - *(hier) wild*
9 **the briefest of moments** - *einen winzigen Augenblick lang*
10 **to blink** - *blinzeln*
11 **edge** - *Ecke*

door, just a few meters away, and he's about to stand and run to it when he hears Penny behind him.

"Lying bastard!" she shouts at him, and her hand reaches across his shoulder, **takes hold of**[1] the knife, and pulls.

Suddenly the pain is even greater, and a **fountain of blood**[2] **sprays**[3] across the elegant hotel room.

Somehow, before she can stab him again, Martin **dives forward and rolls**[4]. He looks back at Penny, who is moving towards him, the knife in her hand, her clothes covered in his blood. "Why, Penny? Why?" he shouts.

The question stops her. "Why? Why? You lying bastard! No bonus? Working in Perth? Who is she? Who's the **tart**[5] you're meeting here? Who's the **high-class hooker**[6] you've been sleeping with?"

"What? Oh god, no! Penny, do you think I'm here with someone else? Oh, you stupid woman. **Don't you see**[7]? This is all for you."

"Liar! I heard the message on our answer phone. Who is she? Some **whore**[8]? Oh Martin, the things she said!" Penny shouts, the wildness still in her eyes.

"A message? What message? There is no other woman!"

"You liar. You're meeting her here! I know you are!

"There is no other woman!"

"And you got your bonus, too! I know you did. You can't lie to me."

"Yeah, I did! That's why I reserved this place for us. For *us, Penny.*"

Penny blinks. "But… you said you were in Perth."

1 **to take hold of sth.** - *etw. (um)greifen*
2 **fountain of blood** - *Blutfontäne*
3 **to spray** - *(hier) spritzen*
4 **to dive forward and roll** - *vorwärts hechten und sich abrollen*
5 **tart (BE, vulg.)** - *Nutte*
6 **high-class hooker (vulg.)** - *Edelhure*
7 **Don't you see?** - *Verstehst du (denn) nicht?*
8 **whore** - *Hure*

"A joke. Just a joke. I **was about to**[1] call you back to tell you. There's a limousine waiting outside our apartment right now. I was going to tell you to get dressed and get in the limo. I wanted to take you out for dinner, to bring you back here. I was going to tell you about the bonus, tell you everything at work is okay now. Oh my god, Penny. Look at me! **What have you done**[2]? You need to call an ambulance, right now!"

"But... but... the message... the other woman." And Martin sees the wildness disappear from her eyes, and his loyal, trusting, obedient wife starts to **reappear**[3].

"There is no other woman. It was some kind of mistake. You need to help me, Penny. Now. I'm dying! Call the ambulance! Get me help!"

"God, what have I done?" she says quietly, and the knife falls from her hands as she moves towards the phone.

"Quickly!" Martin shouts, as he feels the blood continue to **pump**[4] from his shoulder.

But as Penny is about **to lift the receiver**[5], she sees the white gift box that has fallen from the bed to the floor.

The box is now **speckled with red**[6], and **crushed**[7] from their **struggle**[8], but the name tag, Martin sees, is still attached.

He doesn't wait for her to read the message. Before she even reaches to pick it up, he starts **to crawl for the door**[9]. "Help me!" he shouts. "Somebody help me!"

"Susan? Susan? You lying bastard!" he hears his wife scream, and he turns to see her pick up the knife and start to run towards him.

1 **to be about to do sth.** – *gerade etw. tun wollen, beabsichtigen etw. zu tun*
2 **What have you done?** – *Was hast du bloß getan?*
3 **to reappear** – *wieder zum Vorschein kommen*
4 **to pump** – *(hier) quellen; pumpen*
5 **to lift the receiver** – *den Hörer abheben (am Telefon)*
6 **to be speckled with red** – *rot gesprenkelt sein*
7 **to be crushed** – *zerdrückt sein*
8 **struggle** – *Kampf*
9 **to crawl for the door** – *zur Tür kriechen*

And he can't really remember what happens next, but he knows that as she jumps he kicks out his right leg and his foot hits her face. There's the **sound of breaking bone**[1], and he's not sure if it's her nose or her neck, but she falls on top of him and doesn't move again.

He thinks he screams. He thinks he tries to move. He tries to push her body off himself, but he's too weak. His eyes start to close, but he **forces them open**[2], lifts his hand towards the door.

But he can't reach **the handle**[3].

And as the last of his **strength**[4] leaves him, he realizes for the first time that the record is still playing, the needle **skipping**[5], so that the same line is played over and over again.

"All I want for Christmas is... All I want for Christmas is... All I want for Christmas is... All I want for Christmas is...."

The pain in his shoulder is much less now. He feels almost okay. Penny is still on top of him. His wife. Not a bad wife really, he thinks.

His eyes start to close again, and this time he lets them.

Yeah, rest for a minute, he thinks. Get your strength.

And for a moment there is **darkness**[6], and he listens to the line of the song going **round and round**[7]: "All I want for Christmas is... All I want for Christmas is..."

And then he hears the knock at the door.

His eyes open.

He doesn't want to die. Not here. Not like this.

He hears another knock.

The champagne. The bell boy.

"Help me," he says, his voice weak. "Help me."

And the door opens.

1 **sound of breaking bone** – *Geräusch brechender Knochen*
2 **to force sth. open** – *etw. mit Gewalt öffnen*
3 **handle** – *Klinke, Türgriff*
4 **strength** – *Kraft*
5 **to skip** – *hüpfen, springen*
6 **darkness** – *Dunkelheit*
7 **to go round and round** – *sich immer wieder wiederholen*

"All I want for Christmas is..." the song plays.

"You?" he asks, as he looks up at the long-legged, dark-haired woman. "Susan? Thank god. You have to help me."

But the woman at the door doesn't say anything. Instead, she slowly looks around the room, a strange expression in her beautiful dark eyes.

"Susan. You have to be quick. I'm dying."

The woman steps into the room and closes the door behind her.

"Susan? What are you doing?"

Again, for a moment, the woman says nothing. "So, she found you then?" she finally says, and a thin smile **spreads across her lips**[1]. "Well, I'm very **proud of**[2] her. She seemed like such a quiet, gentle woman."

"What? Who?"

"Who? Your wife. Penny."

"Penny? You... you know Penny?"

The woman smiles again. "She doesn't know me, but I know her. The poor thing. I knew you were married the first time you talked to me in that horrible little bar. A woman always knows."

The woman **kneels down**[3] next to Martin. "**For some reason**[4], married men like me. I used to tell them to go away, but **eventually**[5] I realised that I could have a little fun with them. It's so easy. Agree to meet them somewhere. Find out the name and contact details of their wife, then send them a little message and wait for their reaction. **Of course**[6], it isn't always as **impressive**[7] as this, but I always like to come and see the **result**[8]. The message I left for you on your house phone was... well... very detailed. Do you think that's what made her so angry?"

1 **to spread across sb.'s lips** - *sich auf jds. Lippen breitmachen*
2 **to be proud of sb.** - *stolz auf jdn. sein*
3 **to kneel down** - *sich hinknien*
4 **for some reason** - *aus irgendeinem Grund*
5 **eventually** - *letztendlich, irgendwann (einmal)*
6 **of course** - *natürlich*
7 **impressive** - *beeindruckend*
8 **result** - *Ergebnis*

"What? I don't..." But Martin is finding it hard to talk now, and the woman's words are too difficult to understand.

Instead, he watches the woman take a **plastic glove**[1] from her pocket, put it on her right hand, then reach out to touch Penny's neck.

After a minute she **removes her fingers**[2] and smiles. "Good. She's going to be fine."

The woman stands again and looks down at Martin, a large smile on her face. "But I don't think we can say the same about you. Can we, Martin?" And as Martin's eyes start to close for the final time, he sees his one-night-stand turn and leave the room.

And as she closes the door, he hears her start to whistle the **tune**[3] of a familiar Christmas song, and he thinks that he never wants to hear that song again.

And, **as it happens**[4], he never will.

1 **plastic glove** - *Plastikhandschuh*
2 **to remove one's fingers** - *seine/ihre Finger entfernen*
3 **tune** - *Melodie*
4 **as it happens** - *tatsächlich; wie es der Zufall will*

Sydney ist zwar nicht die Hauptstadt Australiens, aber es ist zweifellos die am dichtesten besiedelte Stadt des Landes und wohl auch die bekannteste. In dieser atemberaubenden Metropole befindet sich auch der größte natürliche Hafen der Welt.

Im 18. Jahrhundert befand sich in Sydney allerdings eine der berüchtigtsten Strafkolonien der englischen Krone und erst gegen Mitte des 19. Jahrhunderts wurde Australien durch den Goldrausch als Einwanderungsland entdeckt, wodurch Sydneys kulturelle und wirtschaftliche Bedeutung zunehmend anstieg. Spätestens seit dem Ende des Zweiten Weltkrieges hat sich die Stadt zu einem multikulturellen Zentrum entwickelt. Mittlerweile werden dort angeblich mehr als 250 Sprachen gesprochen und die verschiedensten Kulturen aus aller Welt leben hier in Hochhäusern und familienfreundlichen Vorstadtsiedlungen zusammen.

12. FAITH

There's a **feeling in her guts**[1]. It's the feeling that a religious person might call **faith**[2]. A feeling that all good detectives must listen to.

So she stands in the long grass in the field at the back of the white **wooden**[3] building, a cigarette in her mouth and a **handkerchief**[4] in her hand to wipe the sweat from the back of her neck.

It's hot, a Deep South hot that even a New Orleans detective like Beth Maguire finds **hard to bear**[5].

Or is that just **nerves**[6]?

Because she is nervous. Nervous that she might be wrong. Nervous that she's about to make a terrible mistake.

She moves her hand to the small revolver inside her jacket, but doesn't take it out. She needs to be sure. She needs to **go over**[7] this whole case one more time before she enters that white wooden building.

Mr and Mrs Hall. That's where this all started. That's where this case began.

They were good **folk**[8]; she could see that from the first moment that they walked into her office. Good folk with a bad problem.

The problem was their eighteen-year-old daughter Lucy.

Lucy had **disappeared**[9].

1 **feeling in one's guts** - *Bauchgefühl*
2 **faith** - *Glaube*
3 **wooden** - *hölzern*
4 **handkerchief** - *Taschentuch*
5 **hard to bear** - *schwer zu ertragen*
6 **nerves (Pl.)** - *Nerven*
7 **to go over sth.** - *etw. überprüfen, etw. durchgehen*
8 **folk(s)** - *Leute*
9 **to disappear** - *verschwinden*

The **NOPD**[1] had asked their usual questions and **filed their reports**[2]. They even suggested a **cult**[3] operating in the area around Shell Beach might **be involved**[4]. But when that **trail had ended cold**[5], it seemed like they might never find an answer.

The Halls were **wealthy**[6], **regulars of**[7] their local church, people with important friends. **In short**[8], not the type of people who normally **hire**[9] private detectives like Beth Maguire. But, after two weeks with no news of their daughter, they were ready to look for answers in places the police didn't look; and Beth Maguire had a reputation for finding people.

Some people said it was a talent, others said there was something almost magical about her **ability**[10], but Beth knew that it was a mixture of two things: her years of working as a cop, and the faith she had when she had that feeling in her guts.

"You have to help us. People say you can find anyone." Mrs Hall said. "We have money, and there's no price that's too high."

Her husband was an older man with grey hair and a **worried expression**[11] in his eyes. "These people, this cult, if they have her, if they've taken our little girl..." he said, but the end of his sentence was lost under his wife's tears.

"I'll do everything that I can," Beth replied, and poured the man a glass of water, which he took with a **grateful nod**[12] of the head.

No, these were not the type of people that normally wanted her help, but they were the type of people who probably needed it the most.

"I'll need to see the police reports. I'll need to see your house and speak to Lucy's friends. More importantly, I need

1 **NOPD (New Orleans Police Department)** - *New Orleans Polizeirevier*
2 **to file a report** - *(hier) eine Vermisstenanzeige aufgeben*
3 **cult** - *(hier) Sekte*
4 **to be involved (in sth.)** - *(in etw.) verwickelt sein*
5 **a trail ends cold** - *eine Spur verläuft sich*
6 **wealthy** - *wohlhabend*
7 **to be regulars of sth.** - *(hier) regelmäßige Besucher von etw. sein*
8 **in short** - *kurz gesagt*
9 **to hire sb.** - *jdn. anheuern*
10 **ability** - *Fähigkeit*
11 **worried expression** - *besorgter Ausdruck*
12 **grateful nod** - *dankbares Nicken*

you **to be honest**[1] with me. Remember, I'm not the police. If there was something you couldn't tell them, if Lucy was **mixed up with drugs**[2] or criminals..."

"No, nothing like that!" Mr Hall replied.

"Well, okay. But I need to know everything."

They **agreed**[3], and the case began.

She didn't like the cult **angle**[4] from the start. They called themselves "The Free," a strange name for a strange group. They seemed to like attracting young **followers**[5], but Beth was sceptical that Lucy was the type they wanted.

No, "The Free" looked for followers from the shadows of society: drug **addicts**[6], the **abused**[7], the **mentally unstable**[8].

For a week she looked for another **lead**[9] – a boyfriend that the police had missed, a family secret that no one had spoken about, or a classmate who didn't like Lucy.

But she found nothing.

Finally, she went back to the reports and looked at the information about "The Free" again.

"Why do you think Lucy would be interested in a cult like this, Mrs Hall?" she asked over the phone.

"She wouldn't be: she loved the church. She was a good girl."

"I see, but why did the police start to **investigate**[10] them?"

"**Reverend**[11] Pale mentioned that Lucy had been asking some strange questions. He thought that she was having..." Mrs Hall stopped to cry for a moment.

1 **to be honest** - *ehrlich sein*
2 **to be mixed up with drugs** - *mit Drogen zu tun haben*
3 **to agree** - *zustimmen, einwilligen*
4 **angle** - *Blickwinkel, Perspektive*
5 **follower** - *Anhänger(in)*
6 **addict** - *Süchtige(r); Abhängige(r)*
7 **abused** - *(hier) Missbrauchsopfer*
8 **mentally unstable** - *(hier) psychisch labile Person(en)*
9 **lead** - *(hier) Hinweis, Spur*
10 **to investigate sb.** - *gegen jdn. ermitteln*
11 **reverend** - *Pfarrer, Pastor*

"**Doubts**[1]?"

Yes, the report confirmed that Father Pale was the first one to think there was some connection between these doubts and Lucy's disappearance. When the police **searched**[2] the Halls' house they found her bible. And inside the bible a small **pamphlet**[3] about "The Free."

A pamphlet was not much of a clue, but there was a phone number on it that **had been circled**[4], and when the police checked Lucy's phone, the same number was there in her **dialled numbers**[5].

And Lucy had dialled that number two days before someone saw her getting into a car on a street just a few blocks from her home.

"So, this is why the police stopped looking. It **seemed like**[6] Lucy contacted the cult and went to them **by choice**[7]" Beth said to Reverend Pale a few days later. "I've tried to speak to the leaders of "The Free." I've tried in ways the police **aren't allowed**[8] to. No one is saying anything about Lucy. **To be honest**[9], I don't think that's where she is."

Reverend Pale closed the doors to his church and shook his head. He was a tall man with dark hair, serious grey eyes and a thin mouth. "Yes, I really don't believe that she would go to them. She's a good Christian girl."

"But you think she was having doubts about her religion? That's what you told the police."

The reverend smiled. "No, I told them that she was asking me some difficult questions about her faith. It's not **uncommon**[10] at her age."

1 **doubt** - *Zweifel*
2 **to search sth.** - *etw. durchsuchen*
3 **pamphlet** - *Broschüre, Flugblatt*
4 **to circle** - *umkringeln, einkreisen*
5 **dialled number** - *gewählte Nummer*
6 **to seem like ...** - *scheinen, als ob ...*
7 **by choice** - *freiwillig; aus eigenem Willen*
8 **to be allowed to do sth.** - *etw. tun dürfen*
9 **to be honest** - *ehrlich gesagt, um ehrlich zu sein*
10 **uncommon** - *ungewöhnlich*

The reverend's church was a small **red-brick building**[1] in a quiet part of the city. A nice part of the city, Beth thought as they walked through the garden at the front of the building.

"Of course, I understand. The problem is that she's eighteen. If she did go to the cult by choice, there's nothing the police can do."

Reverend Pale nodded. "I know. Perhaps, if you find her there, I can go to talk to her."

"Yes, maybe. People say that you two **were close**[2]. They say she trusted you. Would you say that, reverend? Did she trust you?"

The reverend stopped and turned to her. "I hope that all of my **flock**[3] trust me, Miss Maguire."

Beth looked into the man's eyes and smiled. "I'm sure they do."

In silence, they walked to the reverend's car, a long green Cadillac parked at the sidewalk in front of her own vehicle. "You're not from New Orleans, are you?" she said.

"No, I'm a country man: from Forrest County. I **guess**[4] you can **tell by my accent**[5]."

"I **bet**[6] you don't have this type of problem up there?" Beth said, lighting a cigarette.

"Well, Miss Maguire," the reverend said with a smile, "you get bad people everywhere, but no, Forrest County is a safe little area. My brother has a beautiful little church there. A fantastic **congregation**[7]. Real believers."

Beth watched the reverend open his car door. "Do you go there very often?"

"No. It's a long drive, and my own flock needs me here."

1 **red-brick building** - *rotes Backsteingebäude*
2 **to be close** - *sich nahestehen*
3 **flock** - *(hier) Schäfchen, Gemeinde*
4 **to guess** - *vermuten*
5 **to tell by sb.'s accent** - *an jds. Akzent hören*
6 **to bet** - *wetten, tippen; schätzen*
7 **congregation** - *(Kirchen)gemeinde*

"I see. Well, thanks for your time. I don't want **to keep you**[1]. It **looks like**[2] you're **heading out of**[3] the city for the night."

"What do you mean?" the reverend asked, and Beth noticed a strange expression on his face.

Beth pointed to the back seat of his car, where there was a bag of clothes.

The reverend smiled. "Ah, no. Those are the clothes that I give to the **homeless**[4]. No, I don't leave the city very often."

"Really?" asked Beth. "I thought someone told me that you didn't **preach**[5] at the church on the last weekend of every month."

The reverend's smile disappeared. "That's true, but only because I work with **charitable organisations**[6] on that weekend."

Beth said nothing for a moment. "It's the last weekend of the month tomorrow."

"Indeed, which is why I really must go, Miss Maguire. I have a lot to do."

"Of course. There's just one more thing. A lot of people say that you say very nice things about Lucy. What exactly about her makes her so special?"

For a moment, there was a strange expression in the reverend's eyes. "That's easy, she's just so… **innocent**[7]."

"Innocent?" asked Beth, and she did not like the sound of the word.

"Yes, like… well, like an angel. There are very few good people in the world these days, but Lucy…" The reverend suddenly stopped speaking. "Anyway, I really must go."

Beth smiled and watched in silence as the reverend got into the Cadillac and started the engine. It was a nice car, but dirty.

1 **to keep sb.** - *jdn. aufhalten*
2 **to look like sth.** - *aussehen, als ob; scheinen, dass*
3 **to head out of sth.** - *(hier) etw. verlassen*
4 **homeless** - *Obdachlose(r)*
5 **to preach** - *predigen*
6 **charitable organisation** - *Wohltätigkeitsorganisation*
7 **innocent** - *unschuldig*

In fact, it looked like it hadn't been washed in months. There was red **dirt**[1] on the **tyres**[2] and bits of long grass **caught**[3] in the **grill**[4]: **signs**[5] of a drive in the countryside.

As she watched the car slowly move away, a feeling began to grow in her guts.

She dropped her cigarette onto the sidewalk and quickly moved to her own car. She opened the door, started the engine, then moved the car into the road.

For a while, she looked for the reverend's car in the traffic in front of her, but saw nothing. Then, in the distance, she saw the back of the green Cadillac. **Carefully**[6], she stayed near to it. After some time, she saw the car move in the direction of the highway, and when she saw the sign for Forrest County she was not surprised. The feeling in her guts was stronger now. She began to think that this case was going to end very soon.

And there was only one question in her mind.

Was she too late to save Lucy?

Now, in the long grass behind the church, she drops her cigarette, checks the **bullets**[7] in her small revolver, hides the **weapon**[8] under her jacket, and walks towards the white wooden building.

There's a sign next to the building that reads "The Church of Angels", and there are six or seven cars outside in the small car park, each one with red dirt from the small Forrest County roads on their tyres.

And there, at the front of the cars, she sees the reverend's long green Cadillac.

1 **dirt** - *Schmutz*
2 **tyre** - *Reifen*
3 **to catch** - *fangen*
4 **grill** - *Kühlergrill*
5 **sign** - *Zeichen*
6 **carefully** - *vorsichtig*
7 **bullet** - *Kugel*
8 **weapon** - *Waffe*

The drive from New Orleans had been long and hot. The reverend drove fast, and twice she nearly lost him. When she finally saw him park at the church, she wanted to follow him straight inside, but her guts told her to wait.

She parked her car further down the road, then walked back to the church through the **woods**[1].

Then she waited, and she watched.

When she saw the first car arrive, she knew she was right to wait. An hour later, when the final car **pulled up**[2], and she saw the driver enter the church and close the door, she knew it was time.

As she reaches the entrance, she hears people **chanting**[3] inside. Quietly, she tries to open the door, but finds that it's **locked**[4].

She takes a step back, lifts her leg, then kicks the door open.

At the front of the church, seven people in white masks and long red **robes**[5] turn to look at her. They are standing in a small circle and there, in the centre of the circle, Beth sees someone **holding a knife**[6] to the throat of a young woman.

"Put the knife down."

The person with the knife **slowly removes their mask**[7], and Beth sees the **familiar**[8] face of Reverend Pale. "You're not welcome here, Miss Maguire" he says, his eyes full of hate and anger. "This is a private ceremony."

"Put it down. This is over."

"Over? No, this is just beginning. We must **make the sacrifice**[9] to the First Angel."

"The First Angel?" asks Beth, her hand moving slowly to her jacket.

1 **woods (Pl.)** - *Wald*
2 **to pull up** - *vorfahren; anhalten*
3 **to chant** - *singen*
4 **to be locked** - *verschlossen sein*
5 **robe** - *Robe*
6 **to hold a knife** - *ein Messer halten*
7 **to slowly remove a mask** - *langsam eine Maske abnehmen*
8 **familiar** - *bekannt, vertraut*
9 **to make a sacrifice** - *ein Opfer bringen*

"Yes, our **true saviour**[1]. The one who will save us from this **fake paradise**[2]. The Lord of Darkness. The Morning Star. The Devil! Lucy is innocent. Lucy will be his sacrifice. She was chosen."

"Yeah, chosen by you. Tell me, reverend, did you put that pamphlet about "The Free" in her bible? Did you ask to use her phone, too? Let me guess, you wanted everyone to think that Lucy had joined "The Free", so no one would look for her too hard."

The reverend says nothing, but a thin smile appears on his face.

"Lucy, are you okay?" Beth asks.

The young girl in the centre of the circle of people has a **gag**[3] in her mouth and her eyes are full of fear.

"Of course she's okay. She's *his* chosen **servant**[4]. And now that you are here, you can be his sacrifice too. Bring her to me!" Reverend Pale shouts to the others in the circle.

Beth **shakes her head**[5]. "I don't think so. **I'm not much of a believer**[6]."

She pulls the revolver from her jacket, and for a second she thinks that she's too slow. The reverend's hand moves, and the knife almost touches Lucy's skin. Then the bullet strikes the reverend in the chest and **knocks him from his feet**[7].

Beth moves forward, her gun still raised, and the other **devil worshippers**[8] turn and run.

Outside, Beth hears the sound of police **sirens**[9], and she knows that they won't get far, so she moves to Lucy and removes the gag from her mouth before moving her away from the body of Reverend Pale.

1 **true saviour** - *wahrer Retter*
2 **fake paradise** - *falsches Paradies*
3 **gag** - *Knebel*
4 **servant** - *Diener(in)*
5 **to shake one's head** - *den Kopf schütteln*
6 **to be not much of a believer** - *nicht wirklich gläubig sein*
7 **to knock sb. from his feet** - *jdn. zu Fall bringen*
8 **devil worshipper** - *Teufelsanbeter(in)*
9 **siren** - *Sirene*

"Are you okay?" she asks the **terrified**[1] girl.

"Yes. Yes, thank you. Thank you so much, the girl says as the tears fall down her face. "It was terrible, but I knew that someone would come. I knew it. I just knew it. I had…"

"Faith?"

Die Bundesstaaten Louisiana, Mississippi, South Carolina, Georgia und Alabama befinden sich in einer Gegend der Vereinigten Staaten, die auch als **Deep South** (Tiefer Süden) bezeichnet wird.

In **New Orleans**, der Hauptstadt von Louisiana, befindet sich die Flussmündung des Mississippi. Die Stadt ist äußerst facettenreich und berühmt für ihre multikulturelle Atmosphäre, das French Quarter und die vielsprachigen Bewohner.

Der Deep South ist bekannt dafür, dass hier der Glaube großgeschrieben wird. – Angefangen vom Katholizismus bis hin zum Glauben an Voodoo findet man hier alle möglichen Glaubensrichtungen. Auf dem Land gelten jedoch traditionelle, religiöse Wertvorstellungen und man stößt hier und da immer wieder auf die typischen weißen Holzkirchen inmitten von grünen Feldern und Wäldern, die das Bild dieser Gegend prägen.

1 **terrified** – *verängstigt*

13. FLESH AND BLOOD

Another **flash of lightning**[1] cuts across the dark, rainy sky, and for a moment the Yorkshire moors are **illuminated**[2].

The trees dance in the wind of the storm, **the rain falls in great sheets**[3] upon the empty fields, but apart from this there is no movement.

Until, that is, a small car appears on one of the thin, **winding roads**[4]. It's an old car, and it moves slowly, almost **as though**[5] **it's afraid of**[6] the storm.

In the driver's seat, a large middle-aged man of about fifty or fifty-five years of age looks out of the **windscreen**[7] and tries to watch the road.

He is tall and fat, with a large grey beard, round face, and friendly green eyes. Occasionally, he reaches forward and uses his hand to **wipe**[8] the windscreen, because the **condensation**[9] makes it difficult for him to see.

When he reaches the top of another hill, he is about to reach forward to wipe the window, when suddenly he sees something in the middle of the road. At first, he thinks that it's just his imagination, but at that exact moment another flash of lightning illuminates the moors again, and he quickly **puts his foot down on the brake**[10].

1 **flash of lightning** - *Blitz(strahl)*
2 **illuminated** - *hell erleuchtet*
3 **the rain falls in great sheets** - *es regnet in Strömen*
4 **winding road** - *kurvige Straße*
5 **as though** - *als ob*
6 **to be afraid of sth.** - *vor etw. Angst haben, sich vor etw. fürchten*
7 **windscreen** - *Windschutzscheibe*
8 **to wipe** - *wischen*
9 **condensation** - *Kondenswasser*
10 **to put one's food down on the brake** - *auf die Bremse treten, (stark) bremsen*

With a screech of the tyres[1] the car comes to a stop, but not before something hits the front of the vehicle.

Not sure about what has happened, he carefully opens the car door and steps out into the night. The wind pulls at his long green coat, and his beard **is** soon **soaked with rain**[2].

He moves to the front of the car, and for a second he sees nothing. Then, at the side of the road he sees a young woman. Her clothes **are covered in blood**[3], there's a large cut on her head, but her brown eyes are wide open and **stare up at**[4] him.

"Help me!" she **screams**[5] in the darkness of the moors. "Please. Please. You have to help me."

For a moment, the man doesn't move. Then, before saying a word, he takes off his coat and moves to her. He puts the coat over her and **kneels down**[6].

"My god!" he says. "I'm so sorry. I didn't see you. What are you doing out here on the moors in this terrible weather?"

"Please," the girl says, and she tries to push herself up from the floor. "We have to go. You have to take me away from here."

"Wait! Be careful. You shouldn't move. You might have broken a **bone**[7]. Look, there's blood all over you."

"No, you don't understand. It's not my blood. I'm okay," she says.

"Not your blood? But I can see a cut on your head."

The girl raises a hand to her head and looks at the red liquid on her fingers. "It's nothing. You have to believe me. Please, you need to take me away from here. There's a man. A terrible man. We have to go."

The driver looks at the girl for a moment, then turns his eyes to the darkness of the moors. "A man? Up here? Who? A friend of yours?"

1 **with a screech of the tyres** - *mit quietschenden Reifen*
2 **to be soaked with rain** - *vom Regen durchnässt sein*
3 **to be covered in blood** - *(hier) blutverschmiert sein*
4 **to stare up at sb.** - *zu jdm. hinaufstarren*
5 **to scream** - *schreien*
6 **to kneel down** - *sich hinknien*
7 **bone** - *Knochen*

The girl tries to stand, but she is too weak. "Please. I'll explain everything. I just need you to take me away from here."

The driver stops and thinks for another moment. His eyes look at the blood on the girl's clothes, then at the terrified expression in her eyes. "Okay, but you're not walking." And he **leans down**[1] and picks her up, his coat still **wrapped around her**[2] like a **blanket**[3].

Without much **effort**[4], he walks back to the car, opens the passenger door, then places her in the seat.

He then turns back to the hills and looks for signs of anyone else.

"Please hurry!" the girl shouts. "We have to go. We have to."

The driver turns away from the wind and rain, gets back into his car, and starts the engine. "We need to get you to a hospital."

"Yes," the girl says, happier now that the car doors are closed. "Yes, and the police. We need to call the police."

As the car starts to move slowly along the road, the driver turns to look at her. She looks like a poor creature **indeed**[5], he thinks, in his large green coat and her bloody clothes. "The police, you say? Has something happened to you, **lass**[6]?"

The girl nods, and suddenly she starts to cry. "Oh god. It was terrible. So terrible. I can't... I don't know how to explain. God, I don't even know where I am," she **sobs**[7].

"Well, lass. I can help you there. You're on the North York Moors. We're on the old road heading towards Middlesbrough. How did you get here? Are you alone?"

"The moors? God. I don't... I don't know," she says, and **fresh tears**[8] fall down her face.

1 **to lean down** - *sich herunterbeugen*
2 **wrap sth. around sb.** - *jdn. mit/in etw. einwickeln*
3 **blanket** - *Decke*
4 **effort** - *Mühe, Anstrengung*
5 **indeed** - *tatsächlich; in der Tat*
6 **lass (ugs., Nordengl.)** - *Mädchen*
7 **to sob** - *schluchzen*
8 **fresh tears (Pl.)** - *neue Tränen*

"Look. It's okay now, lass. We'll get you somewhere safe. But maybe you should try and remember how all this started. You'll need to tell the police."

Another flash of lightning cuts across the sky, and from the corner of his eye the driver sees a strange expression appear on the girl's face. "I was... I was out with my friends. It's Sarah's birthday. We were drinking... dancing."

"Where?"

"Middlesbrough. That's where I live."

"And you drove out here?"

"No, you don't understand. There was a man."

For a moment the driver says nothing. "Go on."

"He... he was in one of the bars. He **came up to me**[1] and tried to talk. At first... well, at first I thought he seemed quite nice. He was tall, with dark hair, handsome. But..."

"But what?" asks the driver, as the car **struggles up another steep hill**[2].

"There was something... strange about him. Something... in his eyes." The girl **shivers**[3], but the driver doesn't think that it is because of her cold, wet clothes. "I told him I wasn't interested. He seemed angry, but he didn't say anything to me. He just turned and walked away."

"And did you see him again?"

The girl thinks for a moment. "Yes. God, yes. We went to another bar, but I saw him behind us. I told one of my friends, but they just laughed."

The girl puts her hand to her head. "I don't... I don't feel well."

"You said you were drinking. Did you drink a lot?"

"No. Not any more than usual," she stops and looks into the darkness. "But after a while I started **to feel strange**[4]. My

1 **to come up to sb. –** *auf jdn. zukommen*
2 **to struggle up another steep hill –** *nur mit Mühe einen weiteren steilen Hügel hinaufkommen*
3 **to shiver –** *zittern*
4 **to feel strange –** *sich unwohl fühlen*

head was **dizzy**[1]. I couldn't **focus**[2]. I wanted to go home, but Sarah and the others were still dancing. I think… I think I went outside for some air… and…"

They reach the top of the hill and below them, far in the distance, they see the town of Middlesbrough.

"And what?" asks the driver.

"He was there! God, I can remember now. I was sick, and I felt someone put their arm around me. Oh god. I remember his voice. He told someone I was his girlfriend. He made a joke; said I was a **lightweight**[3]. I tried to push him away, but I was too… my head… it still feels strange."

"You poor lass. We need to get you to the police **straight away**[4]. **Don't you worry**[5], we'll be there in a few minutes."

The girl **nods her head**[6]. "Thank you. You've saved me. You've saved my life," she says, her eyes full of fear again. "You don't understand what he **was going to do**[7]."

The driver turns to look at her. "What do you mean… do?"

"It was **awful**[8]. I remember his car. At least, I remember he put me on the back seat. I tried to shout. I tried to scream for Sarah, for anyone. But then he was driving. At first, there were lights, but then it was dark, like this."

The car slows a little, the driver **flicks on his right indicator**[9], **hesitates**[10] for a moment, then the car turns onto another road. "You think he brought you all the way up here?"

"Yes, I think so. I don't remember it, but I do remember…" the girl suddenly screams. "Oh god, no!"

"What?" the driver asks.

1 **dizzy** - *schwindelig*
2 **to focus** - *klar sehen; sich konzentrieren*
3 **lightweight** - *Leichtgewicht*
4 **straight away** - *geradewegs, schleunigst*
5 **Don't (you) worry!** - *Keine Sorge!*
6 **to nod one's head** - *mit dem Kopf nicken*
7 **to be going to do** - *(hier) etw. tun wollen*
8 **awful** - *schrecklich*
9 **to flick on the right indicator** - *den rechten Blinker setzen*
10 **to hesitate** - *zögern*

"That place. That awful place. It was like **some sort of factory**[1]. There were dead animals **hanging from hooks**[2] on the **ceiling**[3]. He pushed me past them on a metal chair. I could hear him talking. He called me a pig. He said…" the girl begins to sob again.

"What? What did he say?"

"He said I was just another pig!" she screamed. "And I could see them. The dead pigs. Everywhere. They were hanging from the hooks, the blood **draining from**[4] them."

"It **sounds like**[5] some sort of **slaughterhouse**[6]. Or maybe it was a farm. There's a lot of them up here."

The girl shakes her head. "No. No, he told me what it was. He moved me towards a huge machine. He **pushed a button**[7] and made me watch."

"Watch?"

The girl looks at him with wide, terrified eyes. "He picked up a large **piece of flesh**[8] and he put it into the machine. I didn't want to look, but he **took hold of my head**[9] and he made me."

The car slowly starts to move down a hill into a **valley**[10], and the distant town disappears, its lights lost **beyond the horizon**[11].

"He said, *this is what happens to pigs like you*," she says. "He said, *this is my factory. This is where I bring* **naughty**[12] *pigs. This is where I make…*" for a moment her sobs cover her words and she cries so hard that the driver thinks she might **pass out**[13].

1 **some sort of factory** - *so eine Art Fabrik*
2 **to hang from hooks** - *an Haken hängen*
3 **ceiling** - *(Zimmer)decke*
4 **to drain from sth.** - *aus etw. heraustropfen*
5 **to sound like sth.** - *wie etw. klingen*
6 **slaughterhouse** - *Schlachthaus*
7 **to push a button** - *einen Knopf drücken*
8 **piece of flesh** - *Fleischbrocken, Stück Fleisch*
9 **to take hold of sb.'s head** - *jds. Kopf packen*
10 **valley** - *Tal*
11 **beyond the horizon** - *hinter dem Horizont*
12 **naughty** - *frech; ungezogen*
13 **to pass out** - *ohnmächtig werden*

"**Calm down**[1], lass. Just calm down. It's okay. We're not far away now."

"*This is where… this is where I make my…*"

"What?" "**Sausages**[2]!" she screams. "He said he was going to **make me into**[3] sausages."

The driver says nothing. He doesn't lean forward to wipe the window. He doesn't look at the girl again.

"Oh god. That machine. I can still see it. I can still hear the flesh **being torn to pieces**[4]. I can still smell the blood."

The driver **coughs awkwardly**[5]. "This can't be real, lass. Are you sure it wasn't the drink, or some terrible **nightmare**[6]?"

"It is real!" the girl shouts. "Look at me. Look at my clothes. This isn't my blood. He tried to pick me up, but I was ready for him. I **smashed my head into**[7] his face." She raises her hand to her head again. "I heard him scream. I ran, but he followed me. I couldn't see the door. I was so… so… so scared. I didn't know what to do. I saw… oh god… I saw a large **metal bin**[8]. There was flesh and blood inside it. Pigs. Dead pigs. I knew he was somewhere behind me, so I jumped into the bin. The blood was all over me, but I didn't move. I didn't. I couldn't."

For a moment, the car is silent. Outside, the storm is starting to pass, and the flashes of lightning appear **less frequently**[9].

The car begins to slow down, but the girl starts to speak again.

"I heard him run past me. I heard him open a door. I think he thought **I'd escaped**[10]. I waited. I tried not to think of the smell. Then, after some time, I don't know how long, I got out and went to the door. I thought he was waiting for me, but I ran. I had to. I had to get away from that place."

1 **to calm down** – *sich beruhigen*
2 **sausage** – *Wurst, Würstchen*
3 **to make sb. into sth.** – *jdn. zu etw. machen*
4 **to be torn to pieces** – *in Stücke gerissen werden*
5 **to cough awkwardly** – *verlegen husten*
6 **nightmare** – *Albtraum*
7 **to smash one's head into sth.** – *seinen Kopf gegen etw. schlagen*
8 **metal bin** – *(hier) Metallbehälter*
9 **less frequently** – *seltener*
10 **to escape** – *fliehen; entkommen*

The car finally stops and the driver turns off his engine. The condensation on the windows is so thick now that they can see nothing outside, and there are no sounds but the falling rain and the wind.

The girl looks at him. "I can't remember much after that. Fields. Hills. The rain. Then..." she almost smiles. "Then you... your car. God. I think you saved me. I think you saved my life."

The driver nods his head. "We need to get you inside now. We need to get you out of those wet clothes."

The girl looks down at her clothes and **gasps**[1]. "Oh god. Look at what I've done to your coat," she says. "**It's ruined**[2]."

"It's okay, lass. Don't you worry about that. Don't worry about anything. Not now."

"But there's blood all over it."

And she starts to take the coat off, but suddenly she sees something and stops.

In the darkness of the car, it's hard for her to see exactly what it is: some sort of design on the **chest pocket**[3] of the green coat. "What... what is that?" she says, and she moves her hand across the **embroidery**[4]."These words. What do they say?"

And outside, in the rain, she hears the familiar sound of a door opening, and **footsteps**[5] moving towards the car.

"You have to understand," the driver says quietly. "He's a good **lad**[6] really. He just gets so... so angry. And what can I do? I have to help him. I don't want to. I never want to. But what can I do?" he asks, as the footsteps stop outside the car door. "**After all**[7], he's my own **flesh and blood**[8]."

And as a final flash of lightning cuts across the sky, the girl finally sees the design on the front of the coat.

1 **to gasp** - *nach Luft ringen*
2 **to ruin** - *ruinieren*
3 **chest pocket** - *Brusttasche*
4 **embroidery** - *Stickerei*
5 **footstep** - *Schritt*
6 **lad (Nordengl.)** - *Kerl, Junge*
7 **after all** - *schließlich*
8 **flesh and blood** - *Fleisch und Blut*

"Webber and Son's Sausages" the words say.

But before she can scream, the car door opens, and the nightmare begins again.

→ Die Moore von **North York** erstrecken sich im Norden Englands über ein Gebiet von knapp 1500 km^2 . Die Gegend ist sehr populär, da sich hier unter anderem das größte Heidemoor des Landes befindet. Man kennt es übrigens aus den Harry Potter-Filmen, denn die Szenen mit dem Hogwarts Express wurden auf Teilen der Bahnstrecke des North York Moor Railway mitten im Moor gedreht.

Diese wilde und wunderschöne Moorlandschaft hat selbstverständlich auch eine dunkle, romantische Vergangenheit: Nicht weit davon liegt nämlich die Abtei von Whitby, die Bram Stoker als Inspiration für seinen Roman Dracula diente. Außerdem sind die Moore eine beliebte Gegend für unzählige Geister- und Kriminalgeschichten, da sie vermutlich nicht zu den Orten zählen, an denen man sich gerne nachts verläuft.

WORTLISTE

Verwendete Abkürzungen

AE = *amerikanisches Englisch*
BE = *britisches Englisch*
etw. = *etwas*
jd. = *jemand*
jdm. = *jemandem*
jdn.= *jemanden*
jds.= *jemandes*
Pl. = *Plural*
sb. = *somebody*
sth. = *something*
ugs. = *umgangssprachlich*
vulg. = *vulgär*

	ability	*Fähigkeit*
to be	**about to do sth.**	*gerade etw. tun wollen, im Begriff sein etw. zu tun, beabsichtigen etw. zu tun*
the	**abused**	*(hier) Missbrauchsopfer*
to	**accept an invitation**	*eine Einladung annehmen*
	accident	*Unfall*
	accountant	*Buchhalter(in)*
	acquaintance	*Bekanntschaft*
	actually	*wirklich, tatsächlich*
	addict	*Süchtige(r); Abhängige(r)*
to	**admire sb.**	*jdn. bewundern*
to be	**afraid of sth.**	*vor etw. Angst haben, sich vor etw. fürchten*
	after all	*schließlich; denn*
	After you!	*Nach Ihnen!*
to	**agree**	*sich einig sein; einwilligen, zustimmen*
to	**aim for the head**	*auf den Kopf zielen*
	aisle	*Gang*
to be	**alarmed**	*erschrocken sein*
	all the trimmings (Pl.)	*die ganzen Beilagen; alles, was dazugehört*
	alley	*Gasse*
to be	**allowed to do sth.**	*etw. tun dürfen*
to be	**amazed**	*verblüfft sein, erstaunt sein*
	amazing (ugs.)	*toll*
	an idea begins to form	*allmählich eine Idee haben*
	ancient	*(hier) alt*
	and yet	*aber dennoch, und doch*
	angle	*Blickwinkel, Perspektive*
	angry	*wütend, zornig*
	anniversary	*Jahrestag*
to be	**annoyed**	*genervt sein*
	anyway (ugs.)	*aber egal; jedenfalls*
	apart from	*abgesehen von*
to	**apologise (BE), apologize**	*sich entschuldigen*
to	**appear**	*erscheinen*
	appointment	*Verabredung, Termin*
	arse (vulg.)	*Arsch*
	as it happens	*tatsächlich; wie es der Zufall will*
	as though	*als ob*
to	**assist sb. with sth.**	*jdm. bei etw. helfen*
	at all	*überhaupt*
	at all times	*stets*
to	**attract**	*anlocken*
	auburn	*rotbraun*
to	**avoid sb.**	*jdn. meiden*
	award	*Preis*
to be	**aware that**	*sich bewusst sein, dass*
	awful	*schrecklich*
	bald head	*Kahlkopf, Glatzkopf*
to	**bang one's fists against sth.**	*mit den Fäusten gegen etw. schlagen*
	beard	*Bart*
	bell boy	*Hotelpage*
	beneath	*unter*
to	**bet**	*wetten, tippen; schätzen*
	beyond the horizon	*hinter dem Horizont*
	big drop down there	*hier geht es steil nach unten*

	bill	*Geldschein*
	blanket	*Decke*
to	**blink**	*blinzeln*
	blood pressure	*Blutdruck*
	bloody fool (ugs.)	*dummer Idiot*
	blurred	*unscharf, verschwommen*
	bone	*Knochen*
to be	**bored of sth.**	*von etw. gelangweilt sein*
to	**borrow sth.**	*etw. ausleihen*
	brake	*Bremse*
to	**break the ice**	*das Eis brechen; miteinander warm werden*
	breath	*Atem*
to	**breathe**	*atmen, einatmen*
to	**breathe deeply**	*tief einatmen*
	briefcase	*Aktentasche, Aktenkoffer*
	bucket	*Eimer*
	bucks (Pl., ugs.)	*Kröten (Geld)*
	bullet	*Kugel*
	bulletproof vest	*schusssichere Weste*
to	**burn**	*brennen*
to	**bury sb.**	*jdn. begraben*
	But of course it'll work.	*Aber natürlich wird das klappen.*
	by choice	*freiwillig; aus eigenem Willen*
to	**calm down**	*sich beruhigen*
	calm expression	*ruhiger Ausdruck*
to be	**capable of sth.**	*zu etw. im Stande sein*
	carefree	*sorglos*
	carefully	*vorsichtig*
	carry-on bag	*Reisetasche; Handgepäck*
to	**catch**	*fangen*
	cave	*Höhle*
	ceiling	*(Zimmer)decke*
	CEO (chief executive officer)	*Generaldirektor(in); Geschäftsführer(in)*
	certainly	*sicherlich*
	changing room	*Umkleidekabine; Umkleideraum*
to	**chant**	*singen*
	character	*Person, Wesen*
to	**charge a fee**	*eine Gebühr berechnen*
	charitable organisation	*Wohltätigkeitsorganisation*
	chasm	*Spalte*
	chest	*Brustkorb*
	chest pocket	*Brusttasche*
to	**choose to do sth.**	*etw. freiwillig tun*
to	**chop the body up**	*die Leiche zerstückeln*
	chum	*(hier) Köder*
to	**chum the water**	*das Wasser mit Ködern versehen*
to	**circle**	*umkringeln, einkreisen*
to	**clear sb.'s mind**	*jds. Kopf frei machen*
to be	**close**	*sich nahestehen*
	cloth	*Lappen*
	clue	*Hinweis*
	clumsy	*tollpatschig, ungeschickt*
	coast	*Küste, Ufer*
	coincidence	*Zufall*
	cold case	*ungeklärter Kriminalfall*
	collar	*Kragen*
to	**come up to sb.**	*auf jdn. zukommen*
to	**commit a crime**	*ein Verbrechen begehen*
to	**complain**	*sich beschweren*
	completely psychotic	*völlig psychotisch*
	concern	*Besorgnis, Sorge*
	condensation	*Kondenswasser*
	confession	*Geständnis*
	confident	*selbstbewusst*
	congregation	*(Kirchen)gemeinde*
	connection	*Verbindung*
	consciousness	*Bewusstsein*
to	**consider sth.**	*etw. in Erwägung ziehen, etw. in Betracht ziehen*
	content	*zufrieden*
	contented smile	*zufriedenes Lächeln*
	contents (Pl.)	*Inhalt*
	cops (Pl., ugs.)	*Bullen, Cops*
	corporate espionage	*Wirtschaftsspionage*
to	**cough awkwardly**	*verlegen husten*
	counter	*Theke*
to be	**covered in blood**	*(hier) blutverschmiert sein*
	covered in sweat	*schweißbedeckt*
to	**crawl for the door**	*zur Tür kriechen*
	creatures of habit (Pl.)	*Gewohnheitstiere*
	creep (ugs.)	*Widerling*
to	**cross out sth.**	*etw. ausstreichen*
	cruel	*grausam*
	crunch	*Knirschen*
to be	**crushed**	*zerdrückt sein*
to be	**cuffed together**	*in Handschellen gelegt sein*

	culprit	*Täter(in)*
	cult	*(hier) Sekte*
	cunning	*gerissen, schlau*
	cupboard	*Schrank*
to	**curl into claws**	*sich zu Krallen zusammenrollen*
	curly	*lockig*
	curse	*Fluch*
	customs (Pl.)	*Zoll*
	damn (vulg.)	*verflucht*
	damn thing (vulg.)	*verdammtes Ding*
to	**dare (to) do sth.**	*sich trauen etw. zu tun*
	dark web	*Darknet*
	darkness	*Dunkelheit*
to	**deal in sth.**	*mit etw. handeln*
	Death Cap mushroom	*grüner Knollenblätterpilz*
to	**decorate**	*schmücken*
	delicate lips	*zarte Lippen*
to	**depart**	*abfliegen*
to	**deserve sth.**	*etw. verdienen*
to	**deserve to die**	*es verdienen zu sterben*
to be	**desperate**	*verzweifelt sein*
	desperate kind of laugh	*verzweifeltes Lachen*
	devil worshipper	*Teufelsanbeter(in)*
	devious	*hinterhältig, verschlagen*
to	**dial a number**	*eine Nummer wählen*
	dialled number	*gewählte Nummer*
to be	**difficult to read**	*(hier) schwer zu deuten sein*
to	**dig**	*(hier) sich bohren; sich (ein)graben*
	directly	*genau, direkt*
	dirt	*Schmutz*
to	**disappear**	*verschwinden*
to	**disappoint sb.**	*jdn. enttäuschen*
	disgust	*Ekel*
	disloyal	*treulos, illoyal*
	display case	*Vitrine, Schaukasten*
to	**dispose of sth.**	*sich etw. entledigen, etw. loswerden*
to	**dissolve sth. in acid**	*etw. in Säure auflösen*
to	**distract sb.**	*jdn. ablenken*
	distraction	*Ablenkung*
to	**dive forward and roll**	*vorwärts hechten und sich abrollen*
	dizzy	*schwindelig*
to	**do research**	*Nachforschungen anstellen*
	Don't be too long!	*Brauch nicht zu lang!*
	Don't you see?	*Verstehst du (denn) nicht?*
	Don't (you) worry!	*Keine Sorge!*
to be	**done**	*fertig sein*
	doubt	*Zweifel*
	down-on-their-luck detectives (Pl.)	*abgehalfterte Privatdetektive*
	..., do ya? (ugs., Kurzform von 'do you')	*... oder?*
	dozen	*Dutzend*
to	**drain from sth.**	*aus etw. heraustropfen*
to	**drip**	*tropfen*
	drips of water (Pl.)	*Wassertropfen*
	driving license	*Führerschein*
	drop	*Höhenunterschied, Gefälle*
to	**echo**	*(wider)hallen*
	edge	*Ecke*
	effort	*Mühe, Anstrengung*
	elderly cleaner	*ältere Reinigungskraft*
	embroidery	*Stickerei*
	employee	*Angestellte(r)*
	emptiness and nothingness	*Leere und Bedeutungslosigkeit*
to be	**enchanted**	*entzückt sein, verzaubert sein*
	enthusiasm	*Begeisterung*
	entire	*ganz, gesamt*
	entrance	*Eingang*
to	**escape**	*fliehen; entkommen*
	even if	*selbst wenn*
	eventually	*letztendlich, irgendwann (einmal)*
	every now and again	*ab und zu*
	every now and then	*hin und wieder, ab und zu*
	evidence	*Beweis*
to	**examine sb./sth.**	*jdn./etw. prüfen, jdn./etw. überprüfen; genau ansehen*
to	**exchange sth.**	*etw. austauschen*
to	**exchange doubtful glances**	*skeptische Blicke austauschen*
	exciting	*aufregend, spannend*
to	**exist**	*existieren*
to	**experiment**	*experimentieren*
to	**explode**	*zerbersten, (hier) sich bohren*
	expression	*Ausdruck; Miene; Wendung*

	expression of pain	schmerzhafter Ausdruck
	expression of sadness	trauriger Ausdruck
	extremely poisonous	sehr giftig, hochgiftig
to	fade	(hier) (ver)schwinden
to	fail	versagen
	faith	Glaube
	fake paradise	falsches Paradies
	familiar	bekannt, vertraut
to be	famous (for sth.)	(für etw.) berühmt sein
to be	faster	schneller sein
	fear	Angst, Furcht
to	feed sth. to sth.	etw. an etw. verfüttern
to	feel dizzy	sich schwindelig fühlen
to	feel strange	sich unwohl fühlen
	feeling in one's guts	Bauchgefühl
	figure	Person
	file	Aktenordner, (Akten)mappe
to	file a report	(hier) eine Vermisstenanzeige aufgeben
to be	filled with anger	zornerfüllt sein
to	finally manage to do sth.	schließlich gelingen, etw. zu tun
	fingerprint	Fingerabdruck
to	flash before one's eyes	vor den (eigenen) Augen vorbeiziehen
	flash of lightning	Blitz(strahl)
to	flash one's teeth at sb.	jdm. gegenüber ein Zahnfleischlächeln aufsetzen
	flesh	Fleisch
	flesh and blood	Fleisch und Blut
to	flick on the right indicator	den rechten Blinker setzen
	flight list	Flugliste
	flock	(hier) Schäfchen, Gemeinde
to	fly	fliegen
to	focus	klar sehen; sich konzentrieren
	folder	Aktenordner
	folk(s)	Leute
to be	followed	verfolgt werden
	follower	Anhänger(in)
	footstep	Schritt
	for some reason	aus irgendeinem Grund
to	force sth.	etw. erzwingen
to	force sth. open	etw. mit Gewalt öffnen
	forest	Wald
	fountain	Springbrunnen
	fountain of blood	Blutfontäne
	foyer	Empfangshalle
to be	free to go	gehen dürfen
	fresh tears (Pl.)	neue Tränen
	from the corner of their eyes	aus den Augenwinkeln
to	frown	die Stirn runzeln
	further	weiter
	gag	Knebel
to	gasp	keuchen, nach Luft ringen
	gate	Flugsteig, Gate
	gentle curve	zarte Wölbung
	Georgian	georgianisch
to	get back	zurückkehren; heimkommen
to	get off	aussteigen
	gift (AE)	Geschenk
	gift tag (AE)	Geschenkanhänger, Geschenkschildchen
to	glance at sth.	auf etw. schauen
	glass screen	Glasscheibe
to	go off	losgehen (Alarm)
to	go over sth.	etw. überprüfen, etw. durchgehen
to	go round and round	sich immer wieder wiederholen
to	go through security	die Sicherheitskontrolle passieren
to be	going to do	(hier) etw. tun wollen
to	grab sth.	nach etw. greifen
	grateful nod	dankbares Nicken
	greedy collectors (Pl.)	(hab)gierige Sammler
	grill	Kühlergrill
to	grin	grinsen
to	guess	vermuten; schätzen
	guide	Reiseführer, (hier) Höhlenführer
	guilty	schuldig, schuldbewusst
	habit	Gewohnheit
	handkerchief	Taschentuch
	handle	Klinke, Türgriff
	handsome	gutaussehend
to	hang from hooks	an Haken hängen
to	hang in mid-air	halb in der Luft hängen
	hard to bear	schwer zu ertragen
to	have an affair	eine Affäre haben, fremdgehen
to	have not a scrap of evidence	nicht den geringsten Beweis haben

to	**have people sell sth.**	*(einen) Verkäufer für etw. haben*
to	**have sentimental value**	*(einen) ideellen Wert haben*
to	**have the backbone for sth.**	*das Rückgrat für etw. haben, sich etw. trauen*
to	**have the right to do sth.**	*das Recht haben etw. zu tun*
	head chef	*Chefkoch, Küchenchef(in)*
to	**head out of sth.**	*(hier) etw. verlassen*
	healthy	*gesund*
	heat	*Hitze*
	heirloom	*Erbstück*
	hell, ... (ugs.)	*Mist, .., verdammt ..*
	Hell's Kitchen	*Stadtviertel in Manhattan, New York*
	helmet	*Helm*
to	**hesitate**	*zögern*
to be	**hidden by sth.**	*von etw. verdeckt werden; von etw. versteckt werden*
	hidden switch	*versteckter Schalter*
	high-class hooker (vulg.)	*Edelhure*
	high-heel shoes	*hochhackige Schuhe, Stöckelschuhe*
to	**hire sb.**	*jdn. anheuern*
to	**hold a knife**	*ein Messer halten*
to	**hold out one's hand**	*die Hand ausstrecken*
	homeless	*Obdachlose(r)*
to be	**honest**	*ehrlich sein; ehrlich gesagt, um ehrlich zu sein*
	horrendous	*schrecklich, entsetzlich*
	horrified expression	*entsetzter Gesichtsausdruck*
	however	*jedoch, aber*
to	**hypnotise (BE) sb., to hypnotize sb.**	*jdn. hypnotisieren, jdn. in Hypnose versetzen*
to be	**hypnotised (BE), to be hypnotized**	*hypnotisiert werden*
	hypnotism	*Kunst der Hypnose*
	I bet. (ugs.)	*Bestimmt!, Garantiert!*
	I couldn't help but ...	*Ich konnte nicht anders als ...*
	I don't care	*Es ist mir egal, ...*
	identical	*identisch, genau gleich*
	illuminated	*hell erleuchtet*
	illumination	*Beleuchtung; Lichtquelle*
	immaculate	*makellos*
to be	**impossible to bear**	*unerträglich sein, nicht auszuhalten sein*
	impressive	*eindrucksvoll, beeindruckend*
	in short	*kurz gesagt*
	indeed	*tatsächlich, wirklich, in der Tat*
	innocent	*unschuldig*
to	**inspect sth.**	*etw. untersuchen, etw. überprüfen*
	instead (of)	*stattdessen; statt, anstelle von*
	interview room	*(hier) Verhörraum*
	intimidating	*angsteinflößend*
to	**investigate**	*untersuchen*
to	**investigate sb.**	*gegen jdn. ermitteln*
	investigation	*(hier) Ermittlung*
to be	**involved**	*verwickelt sein, beteiligt sein, mit drin stecken*
to	**iron**	*bügeln*
	jail (AE)	*Gefängnis*
	just	*gerade (eben), erst*
	just in case	*(nur) für den Fall (, dass)*
to	**just open**	*einfach aufgehen*
to	**keep one's voice down**	*leise sein*
to	**keep out of sight**	*sich verstecken; sich versteckt halten, sich nicht sehen lassen*
to	**keep sb.**	*jdn. aufhalten*
to	**keep sb.'s attention on sb.**	*jds. Aufmerksamkeit weiterhin auf jdn. gerichtet halten*
to	**keep sb.'s bed warm**	*jdm. das Bett wärmen*
to	**keep sth. safe**	*etw. sorgfältig aufbewahren*
to	**keep up (with sb.)**	*(mit jdm.) Schritt halten, (mit jdm.) mithalten*
to be	**kept waiting**	*warten gelassen werden*
to	**kill oneself**	*sich (selbst) umbringen*
	kind	*freundlich*
	kind of	*irgendwie*
to	**kneel down**	*sich hinknien, sich niederknien*
to	**knock sb. from his feet**	*jdn. zu Fall bringen*

	lad (ugs., Nordengl.)	*Kerl, Junge*
	lass (ugs., Nordengl.)	*Mädchen*
to	**last longer**	*länger anhalten (Wirkung)*
	laughter	*Gelächter*
	lawyer	*(Rechts)anwalt, (Rechts)anwältin*
	lead	*(hier) Hinweis, Spur*
to	**lean back**	*sich zurücklehnen*
to	**lean down**	*sich herunterbeugen*
to	**lean forward**	*sich vorlehnen, sich nach vorne lehnen*
	less frequently	*seltener*
to	**let sb. go**	*jdn. gehen lassen*
to	**let the wind take sth.**	*den Wind etw. davontragen lassen*
to	**lift the needle**	*die Plattenspielernadel anheben*
to	**lift the receiver**	*den Hörer abheben (am Telefon)*
to	**lift up sth.**	*etw. hochheben*
	lightweight	*Leichtgewicht*
	like sb. owns the place	*als ob jd. der Besitzer wäre*
to	**linger on sb. (eyes)**	*auf jdm. ruhen (Augen)*
	lingerie	*Dessous, Damenunterwäsche*
	lip	*Lippe*
to	**lock up**	*abschließen*
to be	**locked**	*verschlossen sein*
	locker	*Schließfach, Spind*
to	**look extremely confident**	*überaus selbstsicher aussehen*
to	**look into sth.**	*etw. prüfen, etw. untersuchen*
to	**look like (sth.)**	*aussehen wie (etw.); aussehen, als ob; scheinen, dass*
	lot (ugs.)	*Truppe, Haufen*
	luxurious	*luxuriös*
	lying bastard! (vulg.)	*dreckiger Lügner!*
	lyrics (Pl.)	*(Lied)text*
	mad	*verrückt*
	magnet	*Magnet*
	magpie	*Elster*
	mahogany statue	*Mahagonistatue*
to	**make a sacrifice**	*ein Opfer bringen*
to	**make oneself comfortable**	*es sich bequem machen*
to	**make sb. into sth.**	*jdn. zu etw. machen*

to	**make sb.'s blood hot**	*jds. Blut in Wallung bringen*
to	**manage to stand**	*es schaffen zu stehen*
	manic	*(hier) wild*
	mannequin	*Schaufensterpuppe*
	marble bench	*Marmorbank*
	mates rates (Pl., ugs.)	*Freundschaftspreis*
to	**mean**	*bedeuten*
	memory stick	*Speicherstick*
	mentally unstable	*(hier) psychisch labile Person(en)*
	merry	*fröhlich*
	mess	*Durcheinander*
	metal bin	*(hier) Metallbehälter*
to	**mimic sb.**	*jdn. nachahmen*
	mind	*Geist, Kopf; Gedanken*
sb.'s	**mind fills with confusion**	*jd. ist (mit einem Mal) verwirrt*
	minute hand	*Minutenzeiger (an der Uhr)*
to be	**mixed up with drugs**	*mit Drogen zu tun haben*
	modest	*bescheiden*
	mouth	*(hier) Öffnung, Eingang*
to	**move one's fingers over sth.**	*seine Finger über etw. bewegen*
	Ms	*Frau (Bezeichnung, die für verheiratete und für unverheiratete Frauen gilt)*
to	**mumble**	*murmeln*
	muscled	*muskulös*
to	**mutter**	*murmeln*
	naive criminals (Pl.)	*naive Verbrecher*
	nametag	*Namensschild*
	naughty	*frech; ungezogen*
	near the surface	*in der Nähe der Oberfläche*
	Nemain pin	*Anstecknadel bzw. Brosche mit der keltischen Sagengestalt und Göttin Nemain*
	nerves (Pl.)	*Nerven*
	news presenter	*Nachrichtensprecher(in)*
	Nice one! (ugs.)	*Gut gemacht!, Nicht schlecht!*
	nightmare	*Albtraum*

	ninety million dollars' worth of property	*Eigentum im Wert von 90 Millionen Dollar*
to	**nod (one's head)**	*(mit dem Kopf) nicken*
	NOPD (New Orleans Police Department)	*New Orleans Polizeirevier*
to	**not mind sb.**	*nichts gegen jdn. haben*
to be	**not much of a believer**	*nicht wirklich gläubig sein*
	not to make sense/to make no sense	*keinen Sinn ergeben*
to	**notice sth.**	*etw. bemerken*
	now and again	*dann und wann, von Zeit zu Zeit*
	NYPD (New York Police Department)	*New Yorker Polizeirevier*
	obedient	*gehorsam*
	occasional	*gelegentlich*
	of course	*natürlich*
to	**offer**	*anbieten*
	one final piece to the puzzle	*letztes fehlendes Puzzlestück*
to	**only take a minute**	*nur eine Minute dauern*
	overexposed	*überbelichtet*
	overtime	*Überstunden*
to	**owe sb. sth.**	*jdm. etw. schulden*
	pain	*Schmerz*
	pamphlet	*Broschüre, Flugblatt*
	paperwork	*Papierkram*
to	**pass**	*vorbeigehen*
to	**pass out**	*ohnmächtig werden*
	pathetic	*armselig, erbärmlich*
	pathetic worm	*armseliger Wurm, armseliger Wicht*
to	**pay attention to sb.**	*jdm. (seine) Aufmerksamkeit schenken*
	perfect representation	*exakte Wiedergabe*
to	**pick sb. up**	*jdn. abholen*
	piece of flesh	*Fleischbrocken, Stück Fleisch*
	pillow	*(Kopf)kissen*
	pit	*Grube*
to	**plan the whole thing**	*das Ganze planen*
	plastic glove	*Plastikhandschuh*
to	**play dice**	*ein Würfelspiel spielen*
to	**point at sb.**	*auf jdn. zeigen*
to	**point to sth.**	*auf etw. zeigen; auf etw. (hin)deuten*
the	**pommes (vulg.)**	*die Briten*
to	**pour down**	*hinunterfließen, hinunterrinnen*
to	**pour oneself a glass (of sth.)**	*sich ein Glas (...) einschenken*
to	**pour oneself a whiskey**	*sich einen Whiskey einschenken*
to	**preach**	*predigen*
	press	*Presse*
to	**pretend to do sth.**	*so tun als ob man etw. tut, vorgeben etw. zu tun*
to be	**pretty sure**	*sich ziemlich sicher sein*
	prey	*Beute*
	priceless	*unbezahlbar, von unschätzbarem Wert*
	private compartment	*Privatabteil*
	promise	*Versprechen*
to be	**proud of sb.**	*stolz auf jdn. sein*
to	**prove**	*beweisen*
to	**pull up**	*vorfahren; anhalten*
to	**pump**	*(hier) quellen; pumpen*
to	**push a button**	*einen Knopf drücken*
to	**put one's food down on the brake**	*auf die Bremse treten, (stark) bremsen*
to	**put weights on sth.**	*Gewichte an etw. hängen*
	puzzled	*verdutzt, verwirrt*
	quality	*Eigenschaft*
to	**quit**	*aufhören*
to	**raise sth.**	*etw. (hoch)heben, etw. anheben*
to	**ram**	*rammen, stoßen*
to	**reach out one's hand**	*seine Hand ausstrecken*
to	**realise (BE) (that), to realize (that)**	*erkennen (, dass)*
to	**realise sth. (BE), to realize sth.**	*etw. erkennen, sich über etw. bewusst werden*
to	**reappear**	*wieder zum Vorschein kommen*
	recipe	*Rezept*
to	**recognise (BE), to recognize**	*(wieder)erkennen*
	recording device	*Aufnahmegerät*
to	**recreate sth.**	*etw. nachstellen*

	red-brick building	*rotes Backsteingebäude*
	reflection	*Spiegelbild*
to	**refuse**	*ablehnen, sich weigern*
	regret	*Reue, Bedauern*
to be	**regulars of sth.**	*(hier) regelmäßige Besucher von etw. sein*
	relieved	*erleichtert*
	remote	*Fernbedienung*
to	**remove one's fingers**	*seine/ihre Finger entfernen*
to	**reply**	*antworten*
	reputation	*Ruf*
	research	*Recherche, Recherchearbeit*
to	**resist sth.**	*etw. widerstehen*
	result	*Ergebnis*
to	**reveal sth.**	*etw. (her)zeigen, etw. enthüllen*
	reverend	*Pfarrer, Pastor*
	ridiculously expensive	*aberwitzig teuer*
	right under sb.'s nose	*genau vor jds. Nase*
to	**rise elegantly**	*elegant aufstehen*
to	**risk sth.**	*etw. riskieren*
to	**roar**	*brüllen*
	robbery	*Raub(überfall)*
	robe	*Robe*
to	**roll past**	*(hier) vorbeiziehen*
	row	*Reihe*
	rubbish	*Müll*
to	**ruin**	*ruinieren*
	satisfied smile	*zufriedenes Lächeln*
	sausage	*Wurst, Würstchen*
	sb.'s mind fills with confusion	*jd. ist (mit einem Mal) verwirrt*
	scar	*Narbe*
	scarred and tattooed body	*vernarbter und mit Tätowierungen übersäter Körper*
	scene of the crime	*Tatort*
	scream	*Schrei(en), Geschrei*
to	**scream**	*schreien*
to	**scribble on sth.**	*auf etw. kritzeln*
	scruffy writing	*schlampige Schrift*
to	**search sb./sth.**	*jdn./etw. durchsuchen*
	security guard	*Wachmann, Sicherheitsbeamter, -beamtin*
	seductive	*verführerisch*
to	**seem calm**	*ruhig erscheinen*
to	**seem genuinely confused and afraid**	*wirklich verwirrt und eingeschüchtert erscheinen*
to	**seem like ...**	*scheinen, als ob ...*
	seemingly endless	*scheinbar endlos*
to	**send a shiver down one's spine**	*jdm. einen Schauer über den Rücken jagen*
	sensual	*sinnlich; erotisch*
to	**separate**	*abtrennen*
	serial killer	*Serienmörder(in)*
	servant	*Diener(in)*
	serviette	*Serviette, Stofftaschentuch*
to be	**set (novel)**	*stattfinden, (hier) spielen*
	setting sun	*untergehende Sonne*
	several sightings (Pl.)	*einige Beobachtungen*
	shadow	*Schatten*
to	**shake**	*(hier) beben*
to	**shake one's head**	*den Kopf schütteln*
	shape	*Gestalt, Form*
to	**shiver**	*zittern*
to	**shrug**	*mit den Schultern zucken*
to	**sigh heavily**	*schwer seufzen*
	sign	*Zeichen*
	sign of nervousness	*Zeichen von Nervosität*
to	**silence**	*dämpfen (Schall)*
to	**silence sb.**	*jdn. zum Schweigen bringen*
	silly	*dumm*
	silver necklace	*silberne (Hals)kette*
	similar	*ähnlich*
	sinister	*düster, finster*
	sip	*Schluck*
	siren	*Sirene*
	skill	*(hier) Geschicklichkeit*
to	**skip**	*hüpfen, springen*
	skyscraper	*Wolkenkratzer*
to	**slam sth. down**	*(hier) etw. hinknallen*
to	**slap sb. across the face**	*jdm. ins Gesicht schlagen, jdm. eine klatschen*
	slaughterhouse	*Schlachthaus*
to	**slip**	*ausrutschen*
to	**slip into a seat**	*in einen Sitz hineinrutschen*
to	**slowly remove a mask**	*langsam eine Maske abnehmen*
to	**slowly spill**	*langsam herausfließen*

to	smash one's head into sth.	seinen Kopf gegen etw. schlagen
	smooth plastic mask	weiche Plastikmaske
to	smuggle	schmuggeln
to	snap	blaffen, schimpfen
to	snap open	aufschlagen
to be	soaked	patschnass sein
	soaked in sweat	schweißgebadet
to be	soaked with rain	vom Regen durchnässt sein
to	sob	schluchzen
	solicitor	Rechtsanwalt, -anwältin
to	solve a crime	einen Fall lösen
	some sort of factory	so eine Art Fabrik
	something extremely terrible	etwas ganz Fürchterliches
to	sound like sth.	wie etw. klingen
	sound of breaking bone	Geräusch brechender Knochen
	sous-chef	stellvertretende(r) Küchenchef(in), Souschef(in)
to be	speckled with red	rot gesprenkelt sein
to	spill out	(hier) (heraus)quellen
to	spill sth. onto sth.	etw. auf etw. (ver)schütten
	spot	(hier) Ort, Platz
to	spray	(hier) spritzen
to	spread across	sich breitmachen über, sich ausbreiten über
to	spread across sb.'s lips	sich auf jds. Lippen breitmachen
	spy movie	Spionagefilm
to	stab into sth.	in etw. stechen
	stab of anxiety	Anflug von Unsicherheit, Anflug von Panik
to	stab sb. in the chest	jdn. in die Brust stechen
	stab wound	Stichwunde
to	have been stabbed a dozen times	mehrere Dutzend Stichwunden erlitten haben
	stalactite	Stalaktit, Tropfstein
	stalagmite	Stalagmit, Tropfstein
to	stand up and stretch	aufstehen und sich strecken
to	stare up at sb.	zu jdm. hochstarren
to	steal	stehlen
to	steal from sb.	jdn. bestehlen
	sth. is supposed to be sth.	etw. soll etw. sein
	stomach	Magen
	stool	Hocker
	straightaway, straight away	sofort, sogleich; geradewegs, schleunigst
to be	strangled	erdrosselt werden
	strength	Kraft
to	stretch out	sich erstrecken
to	strike	(hier) aufschlagen
	struggle	Kampf
to	struggle to do sth.	sich schwertun etw. zu tun; damit kämpfen etw. zu tun
to	struggle up another steep hill	nur mit Mühe einen weiteren steilen Hügel hinaufkommen
	study	Arbeitszimmer
to	stumble	stolpern
	stupid coward (ugs.)	dummer Feigling
to	suggest sth.	etw. vorschlagen
	suicide	Selbstmord
	suitcase	Koffer
to be	supposed to do sth.	etw. angeblich tun sollen
	sweat	Schweiß
to	sweat and bleed	sich abrackern
	sweetheart (ugs.)	Schätzchen
	swords and daggers	Schwerter und Dolche
to	take a cloth from one's apron	ein kleines Tuch aus der Schürze nehmen
to	take a deep breath	tief einatmen
to	take hold of sb.'s arm	jdn. am Arm packen
to	take hold of sb.'s head	jds. Kopf packen
to	take hold of sth.	etw. (um)greifen
	tangled mess	zerzaustes Durcheinander
	tanned	braun gebrannt, sonnengebräunt
	tanned skin	sonnengebräunte Haut
to	tap against sth.	gegen etw. tippen
	tart (BE, vulg.)	Nutte
	tear	Träne
to	tell by sb.'s accent	an jds. Akzent hören
	terrified	verängstigt
	terrifying	furchterregend

	the briefest of moments	*einen winzigen Augenblick lang*
	the last thing sb. needs	*das Letzte, was jd. braucht*
	The rain falls in great sheets.	*Es regnet in Strömen.*
	the slightest scent of sth.	*(ein) zarter Hauch von etw.*
	the tiniest of cracks	*ein klitzekleiner Spalt*
	theft	*Diebstahl*
	their own guns raised	*mit erhobenen Waffen*
	thief	*Dieb(in)*
	thin ledge	*schmaler Felsvorsprung*
	thinning brown hair	*schütteres braunes Haar*
	(this) very	*eben dies(-e, -er)*
	though	*jedoch*
	thought	*Gedanke*
	throat	*Kehle*
	tide	*Gezeiten, (hier) Flut*
to	**tighten with anxiety**	*sich vor Sorge zusammenziehen*
	tile	*Fliese*
	tip	*Trinkgeld*
	tone of voice	*Tonfall*
	tongue	*Zunge*
to be	**torn to pieces**	*in Stücke gerissen werden*
	tower block	*Hochhaus*
	A trail ends cold.	*Eine Spur verläuft sich.*
to be	**trapped**	*(hier) eingeklemmt sein*
	trickle of blood	*dünner Blutfaden*
to	**trip**	*stolpern*
to be	**trouble**	*für Unruhe sorgen, Schwierigkeiten bedeuten*
	true saviour	*wahrer Retter*
to	**trust sb.**	*jdm. (ver)trauen*
	trusting	*treuherzig, vertrauensselig*
	truth	*Wahrheit*
	tune	*Melodie*
to	**turn the volume down**	*etw. leiser stellen*
to	**twinkle**	*funkeln; glitzern*
	two-way glass	*Einwegspiegel*
	tyre	*Reifen*
	umbrella	*Regenschirm*
	unbreakable	*unzerbrechlich*
	uncommon	*ungewöhnlich*
	unconsciousness	*Bewusstlosigkeit*
	underwear	*Unterwäsche*
	unfortunately	*leider*
	unless	*außer*
	unmistakeable	*unverwechselbar, eindeutig*
	unreadable expression	*(Gesichts)ausdruck, der sich nicht deuten lässt*
	valley	*Tal*
	Variety is the spice of life.	*Abwechslung gibt dem Leben erst die (nötige) Würze.*
	vast	*riesig*
	victim	*Opfer*
	viewpoint	*Aussichtspunkt*
	villain	*Schurke, Verbrecher(in)*
	waist	*Taille*
to	**walk all over sb.**	*jdn. schikanieren, jdn. ausnutzen*
	wallet	*Geldbörse, Brieftasche*
	warm breeze	*warmer Lufthauch*
	wealthy	*wohlhabend*
	weapon	*Waffe*
	weathered	*wettergegerbt*
	well-dressed	*gut gekleidet*
	What have you done?	*Was hast du bloß getan?*
	what sth. is all about	*wovon etw. handelt, worum es bei etw. geht*
	wheelchair	*Rollstuhl*
to	**whisper**	*flüstern*
to	**whistle**	*pfeifen*
	Who cares?	*Wen kümmert es?*
	whore	*Hure*
	wide-shouldered	*breitschultrig*
	winding road	*kurvige Straße*
	windscreen	*Windschutzscheibe*
to	**wipe**	*wischen*
to	**wipe the tears away**	*(sich) die Tränen wegwischen*
	with a screech of the tyres	*mit quietschenden Reifen*
	wooden	*hölzern*
	wooden terrace	*Holzterrasse*
	woods (Pl.)	*Wald*
	worried expression	*besorgter Ausdruck*
to	**wrap sth. around sb.**	*jdn. mit/in etw. einwickeln*
to	**wriggle through sth.**	*mit Mühe über etw. klettern, sich durch etw. hindurchwinden*
	Yeah right! (ugs.)	*Ja klar!*
	You don't get to ...	*Du wirst nicht/Sie werden nicht ...!*